For Winners Only

Jimmy —

hold on to this !

[forever]

Tony

For Winners Only

Peter J. Andrews

A Citadel Press Book
Published by Carol Publishing Group

A Citadel Press Book
Published by Carol Publishing Group

Citadel Press is a registered trademark of Carol Communications, Inc.
Editorial Offices: 600 Madison Avenue, New York, NY 10022
Sales & Distribution Offices: 120 Enterprise Avenue, Secaucus, NJ 07094
In Canada: Canadian Manda.Group, One Atlantic Avenue, Suite 105, Toronto, Ontario, M6K 3E7, Canada
Queries regarding rights and permissions should be addressed to: Carol Publishing Group, 600 Madison Avenue, New York, NY 10022

Manufactured in the United States of America
ISBN 0–8065–1728–X

Carol Publishing Group Books are available at special discounts for bulk purchases, for sales promotions, fund raising, or educational purposes. Special editions can also be created to specifications. For details contact: 120 Enterprise Avenue, Secaucus, NJ 07094

12 11 10 9 8 7 6 5 4 3 2 1

Library of Congress Cataloging-in-Publication Data

Andrews, Peter J.
  For winners only : the only casino gambling guide you'll ever need Peter J. Andrews.
      p.   cm.
  "A Citadel Press book."
  Includes index.
  ISBN 0-8065-1728-X (pbk.)
  1. Gambling systems. 2. Games of chance (Mathematics) I. Title.
GV1302.A55   1995
795'.01—dc20   95-20989
                                             CIP

LADY LUCK

You had a single buck to start
and had the feeling in your heart.
The game you chose was good old Craps—
you knew the odds and all the facts.

Like a pro you broke banks in Vegas,
you knew all the Alphas through the Omegas.
But there was one thing you failed to see
that Lady Luck was the winning key.

Before you counted all the money,
you bought some booze and a little honey.
You dropped it all in a single night—
and now I hope you've seen the light.

So now be always on your toes,
'cause lady luck just comes and goes.
Thus, you won't have to starve much longer
'cause lady luck is around the corner.

Once you're back in the chips again,
forget the booze and the lady friend.
So bet it all and let it ride—
but "only" when lady luck is on your side.

Contents

About the Book
and Its Author

Men and women have gambled since time immemorial and continue
to do so, both in wagering and in daily life.

Have I gambled during the last three decades? You can bet all
your possessions, including your bottom dollar, on it. But I gambled
gracefully to some dreadful losses, and then built my gambling stakes
back up to astounding levels which would satisfy even the most
wealth-worshipping but envious casino employee. My wins and
losses consistently advanced in size through the years—surprising
even me—as time after time I was led to conclude that casino
gambling success could end even for someone with extraordinary
knowledge of the major games. In the end it happened to me, just as
it did to several other professional gamblers, and at more than one
casino.

Humbleness is a common virtue in our world, thus I shall not
press this issue by describing the highlights of my gambling career.
The various true stories told here should cast a light on my
capability, character, and performance in private gambling sessions
and at casino tables. Many top-rated gamblers, as well as casino
personnel have questioned the source of my abilities.

Regardless of what took place during my highrolling era, the time
has come for me to reveal the secrets which I have accumulated
since the early 1960s.

Plato, the ancient Greek philosopher, once said: "If we continue to ask the proper questions, we shall obtain the answers to all our dilemmas."

When it comes down to winning at the tables, you can stop asking questions this instant, because for years I've asked myself enough questions for all of us. This book is a gambler's primer and should be read by anyone who intends to approach a casino table.

If you have gambled at private games or casino tables, you have won and probably mostly lost, as have millions of other players. A quick look back and a precise calculation of your own capabilities should indicate whether you qualify to be a successful gambler. In addition, computation of your losses will never be accurate till your first compound all the rake, juice, or house percentage and then deduct it from your loss figures. The type of game you played, and if there was cheating involved, should also be considered and then deducted from your losses.

Unfortunately, gambling and cheating are usually connected, and cheating is probably a cause of some of your losses. If during your visits to specific casinos, you noticed flipping of the dice by stickmen at Craps, you may be assured that this procedure was not always accidental. This may have cost some of you relatively small losses, but there are others less fortunate, who have paid dearly because of the flipping of the dice during certain games. (It is difficult to win consistently against the power of the stick.)

Throughout my gambling career, I've made bets ranging from one dollar to more than $10,000, where the house limit permitted, and higher in private action, to see the outcome determined by a single point at Craps or by the turn of a single card. I have won and lost more than a conservatively estimated figure of $200,000,000 in private and casino action. The amount mentioned, however, is no record when we consider professional gambling involvement. A big bettor can easily turn over $100,000, or even more, in a period of a single day or night at the tables.

Most of the winning methods, which are explained in detail in the following chapters, have been my secrets for many years. I now offer them to you, the player who may have suffered previous losses, so that you may turn the tables on the casinos and go home with some of *their* money.

The following chapters were written to teach you how not to become a professional loser. For too long I've watched players who considered themselves knowledgeable lose their last dollar and sometimes their cars, homes, even their families. The ways to win are clearly presented and, with a few simple moves, will allow the bettor to take full advantage of casino odds.

As you read, various systems may at first appear difficult to understand. However, I have tried to explain my methods as carefully and simply as possible.

Introduction

Once, on a hot July day, I was riding in a cab from McCarran International to the Las Vegas Strip. The temperature had to be over 110 degrees. Heat waves rising from the hot asphalt were almost the equivalent of a mirage. The sight of the Las Vegas hotels with their palm trees, the advertising signs, and the people walking just didn't seem real. The thought crossed my mind that in this oasis, the hotels were desert palaces, and the people wandering around had dreams of possessing the kingdom. The hotels, however, were palaces made of sand. Thus the public's dream was unrealistic because most of them had only a rudimentary knowledge of the various games played in the kingdom. I thought of previous trips, when I departed Las Vegas with nearly empty pockets. I also thought of winning visits, when I had so many $100 bills on me that I experienced the feeling of having conquered the world. As I continued to muse, the fact that the odds were against me preyed on my mind. Each casino that I passed along the Strip offered different memories. Reminders of triumphs and catastrophic losses. The $10,000 in my hip pocket, which had given me a sense of strength and confidence when I left Denver, seemed to lessen in value considerably in the Las Vegas heat. As tires squealed, a sudden stop of the taxi jostled me back to reality.

The cab driver began to yell at the driver in front of us, who had stopped suddenly at a red light.

"Watch what you're doing, jerk! Can't you drive? Where did you get your driver's license...out of a slot machine?" the cab driver added, following some unrepeatable profanity.

The line used by the cab driver was so humorous I had to chuckle. "What's wrong?" I asked, even though I knew that he had been following the car ahead too closely.

"Oh, that damn jerk had plenty of time to make the light, but instead he slammed on his breaks," the driver answered, seeking my approval. "I've driven you around this town before, Pete...and you know how carefully I drive. How are you doing against these joints? I'm still waiting to read in the news that you finally broke one of them!"

"If they had open limit, a person could actually win a big chunk," I said, grinning. "But with the house limits, you'll never hear of anyone breaking a casino!"

"I guess you're right, Pete...they sure got things figured out," the cab driver said in disgust. "They're not taking any big risks...that's for damn sure!"

Before long, the cab pulled up to the entrance of the hotel where I had reservations. When I passed through the doors, the atmosphere inside was familiar as always. The clanging of the machines and the people milling around created the usual pandemonium.

I walked to the front desk and checked in. Turning over my luggage to the bellman along with a tip, I asked him to take the bags upstairs. I couldn't face the casino and the gambling just yet, so I thought of stopping in the coffee shop for a piece of mocha cake and some coffee. Perhaps the sugar in the dessert would generate enough energy to allow me to face the odds and the dealers in a more relaxed mood. The snack seemed to work, because soon I was at a Craps table and very much involved.

I began to bet on the Don't Pass and occasionally on the Don't Come. This particular procedure can actually turn the minus casino odds in Craps to a plus expectancy. (It's my favorite way to operate. This wagering technique has accounted for the bulk of my casino winnings.)

Before a shooter throws the dice, I make a Don't Pass bet. Suppose the shooter tosses a 6? I make a Don't Come bet. Next, if the shooter throws a 4, I lay odds against the 4 and wait till the shooter rolls a 7. If he doesn't, and he repeats the 6, then it is unlikely that he'll repeat the 4. If he also repeats the 4, I follow up with two more Don't Come bets. In this case let's assume he throws a 5 and a 10. I lay odds against the 5 and the 10, that they don't repeat. If the shooter sevens out, my two wins bring me a little profit, and I come out ahead on this transaction. But let's suppose that the dice go really crazy and he also repeats the 5 and the 10. In order for a pair of dice to perform such apparent miracles the shooter must have tossed them at least fifteen or twenty times. I chase the four numbers lost, by betting the Don't Come each time the dice are tossed, but at the same time doubling the size of bets. Now, let's assume the shooter throws a 6, then a 10, then a 5, then a 9, then a 4, and then an 8. The bases are loaded. If he now tosses a 7, even this late in the count, I have a generous profit because I get paid on all the numbers. With this system, that's six winning numbers, versus the previous four that I lost. (When I bet the Don't Pass and the Don't Come, I lay odds against all the points, which are 4, 5, 6, 8, 9, 10.) We must also consider how many times I win by betting this way on short rolls—when the shooter does not repeat the two original bets. In addition, if the first bet made (the original Don't Pass) had been any 4, 5, 9, or 10, the shooter would have had a longer-odds number to repeat. There really isn't any reason for a second bet on the Don't Come. I simply wait till the shooter repeats it, or most likely sevens out. If the first number tossed is either a 4 or a 10, better yet. The odds are 2 to 1 in my favor. Odds are 2 to 1 that the shooter will not repeat either of those two numbers.

I was in my first hour of playing and was ahead around $5,000. The on-going comments from the pit bosses, and even the casino manager, were escalating. From my left, I heard the casino manager tell the pit boss that he didn't like the way I was betting, and it was purposely said loud enough for me to hear. This comment made me want a drink, but this wasn't the proper time. To my right, an old lady had walked up and asked me to explain the exact way I was betting, and why I was winning so much.

"Ma'am, you've got to be kidding." I answered nervously, still thinking of the casino manager. "I'm betting too fast and too high to be taking time off to explain. Why don't you buy some chips and follow my lead? You never know...you may even win a little!

"That's what I need to do, is win," her voice cried out, and then she reached for my forearm. "You don't know this, sir...but I have many big bills to pay. My husband has been in the hospital for two months!"

"Doesn't Medicare cover the costs of hospital bills?" I asked, not yet sure whether I was being hustled.

"Not all of them!" she answered, as she took my advice and bought $50 worth of chips.

Approximately three hours later—with my help in several sizable bets (and advice)—she was about $2,000 ahead. My own winnings surpassed $25,000.

I sensed that the hostility from the pit bosses was peaking, so I asked the payoff man to bring all my bets down, except for the number 4, because of the 2 to 1 edge.

I asked for the hotel's security to bring some racks to fill with my chips, and to cash in. The old lady was extremely grateful. My one concern about her was that she had not won enough to pay the hospital bills. The dealers were now smiling, expecting their usual sizable tips. To their dismay, I counted out thirty black chips ($3,000) and handed them to the lady.

"The boys of this table are donating their tips to you ma'am...toward your husband's hospital bills!" I said. "We all wish him the very best!"

I stayed away from that particular casino from then on.

For Winners Only

Chapter 1

The New World

I was born in 1942 in Athens, Greece, where my father was a coffee merchant. He dealt with traders in Europe, South America, and the continental United States.

My recollection begins with my witnessing the destruction caused by World War II in Athens. Accompanying my parents on trips throughout Greece, I saw derailed trains, demolished buildings, and burned homes, the sight of which will remain in my mind forever.

My father was captured twice during those wartorn years, first by the Nazis and later by the Communist guerrillas. On both occasions he was detained and nearly executed for helping hungry countrymen and several Jewish refugees who had fled their countries and moved to Greece for safety. My father's coffee mills were also busy grinding wheat and corn during those years, since people were starving because of the lack of food production in Greece and most of Europe. When he was captured by the Nazis, my mother, in her grief, gathered together several ordinary citizens my father had helped in the past. They testified that he was not taking sides, but only aiding starving people. This saved him from the firing squad. A few years later, when my father was captured by the Communist guerrillas, he was recognized by their leader. This commanding officer had never forgotten my father, who had once picked him up off the sidewalk when he was starving during the previous Nazi war. (My father, who couldn't bear anyone's suffering, had given him food and flour, saving him and his family from starvation.)

At the war's end, there were endless accounts of brave Greek warriors who fought against Italy, Germany, and then the Communists.

Since my early years I had been strongly influenced by my father's admiration for Greek philosophy, which for most of his years remained the basis of his outlook on life. He so sparked my interest, that by the time philosophy lessons were available to me in the fifth grade, I was eagerly reading my sister's seventh grade books. My interest in *seeking truth* actually began at an early age. During the day I attended a private school in Athens, and each evening my sister, brother, and I were tutored by a governess in the Greek, English, and French languages.

Fearing another war in Greece, in 1955 my parents decided to move to America, where we had relatives and friends. Because we loved Greece, we extended our vacation plans and first visited other areas of our country. However, our visits to several cities took longer than expected. As a result, our Greek oceanliner tickets expired, and our visas were to expire the next day. Having no choice, we had to depart overnight on the Italian liner *Saturnia*, from the harbor of Patra.

When we left Greece in December of 1955, we wore summer clothing because it was a warm, sunny day. Our first stop was Sicily, where there was similar weather. No sooner had the *Saturnia* docked than peddlers rushed aboard, selling watches to passengers which stopped running in less than 48 hours and jewelry that oxidized before the end of the trip. We left the ship for a short period and enjoyed a walk among the shops within the harbor-piazza of Palermo. Our second stop was Naples, a beautiful seaport town with Mt. Vesuvius in the background. In Naples we bought additional souvenirs for relatives and friends we would soon meet in America. Two days later, our ship passed the Rock of Gibraltar. Our last stop before crossing the ocean was Lisbon, Portugal.

Leaving Europe behind on New Year's Eve, our ship was accompanied by dolphins for part of the four-day journey across the vast Atlantic. Crossing the ocean seemed endless. I remember exploring the ship along with my younger brother. We scouted each level, including the engine room and even the kitchen, where we became friends with one of the chefs. He, with his broad, inviting smile, waved us in and made us welcome by filling our hands with pastries. After dark we walked the ship's deck, where we would see vessels from America headed towards Europe. The blinking lights on the other ships, sending flashing Morse code, would capture our attention. My brother and I tried to answer their signals with our flashlights, but by using our own *special code* which included red and green flashes.

Early one morning, while it was still dark outside, we were awakened by loud blasts that signaled the arrival of *Saturnia* in the harbor of Halifax, Canada. Excitement was great, since we knew that we would soon land. To our surprise, there was nearly two feet of snow to welcome us in Halifax. Quite an experience. We had to seek special permission to get into our luggage, since we were not prepared for weather of that nature. We nearly all froze as we walked around the harbor. "All," of course, means my family. The family included the young female dachshund "Sherley" (named after Shirley Temple) we brought from Athens. Sherley appeared to love the new world immediately.

The following morning as the ship neared our American destination we strained, to no avail, to catch through the fog a glimpse of the Statue of Liberty. I looked over the railing and saw that the *Saturnia* was being pulled by tugboats up the New York harbor, via a path cut through thick sheets of ice floating on the Hudson River.

No sooner had the ship docked than Uncle Milton and Aunt Helen (our mother's sister and her husband) were on board returning the favor my father had done for them when they visited Greece. They escorted us ashore, eliminating lengthy customs inspections. I thought Uncle Milton must have great connections. He had to be a well known figure in the area.

On our first day, Uncle Milton arranged a quick tour of New York. I was impressed with the skyscrapers and with the cars driven over the high bridges and through the tunnels under the Hudson river to New Jersey.

Uncle Milton owned several houses, apartment buildings, and a beautiful home on Long Island. For the first few weeks we enjoyed tours to upstate New York, Long Island, and New Jersey. Our cousins, who were much older, entertained us at restaurants, clubs, and Radio City more than once. I liked New York so much that I wanted to live there sometime. I even remember my first root beer and will always recall the taste.

"It tasted awful!" my sister and I agreed instantly. "That liquid had to be made of iodine!"

In February, accompanied by Uncle Milton, we departed from Newark, New Jersey, by train. Our destination, this time, was Cheyenne, Wyoming. That's where my father's four brothers and their families lived. The Andrews family was one of the wealthiest in Wyoming. I distinctly remember gazing out of the train's window along with my sister and brother. At times, our noses pressed the glass, as our eyes searched the endless plains for cowboys. Although the only description we had of them was what we had seen in movies, we knew they lived in the Great West where we would make our new home. Once, my younger brother even said he saw *real live Indians* when my sister and I weren't looking.

Late the following evening, our relatives welcomed us at the Cheyenne train station and drove us to their restaurant, which was only two blocks away. It was the most amazing two-block ride we ever had. It must have snowed a foot. We couldn't believe the car could drive over the snowpacked streets.

The Mayflower Restaurant and Saloon, which was owned by my uncles since 1928, was known from Omaha to the West Coast. The colorful advertising sign displayed a well-lighted ship with sails, the original *Mayflower* on which the Pilgrims sailed to America. There was a big porthole on each side of the entrance to the huge restaurant. When we entered the café area, I noticed it was designed to resemble a ship's tavern with a long counter, an oyster bar, and many booths. As we walked on, we heard live western music and singing, so we peeked into the saloon. We noticed stuffed buffalo, deer, and elk heads hanging on the walls. Finally, we saw real cowboys, many of them wearing hats, boots, and all the works standing at the long bar. Toward the rear of the restaurant there was a large dining room. A sign in Old English lettering over the entrance read *The Marine Room*. This room appeared large enough to seat one-hundred people. That's where a long banquet table was set up and reserved for our party. The decor was designed to resemble the deck of an old ship with masthead, captain's steering wheel, and compass. The entire room was surrounded by a railing resting on carved posts.

For a moment, the room made me feel I was back on the ocean again instead of being 1,600 air-miles inland. My relatives were as warm and friendly as they had been in Greece when visiting us.

It was easy to adjust to our new life-style, although Cheyenne was a small town. At school, some of the kids called me "Pete the Greek." (Quite a change from Pänos Demetrius Andreas. I really enjoyed being called a Greek.)

One day, however, my brand new red three-speed bicycle was stolen. A few days later it was recovered by Cheyenne Police and was returned with a coat of black paint on it. Not too long after that experience, I decided to go back East and visit Aunt Helen and Uncle Milton.

Between the ages of fourteen and eighteen I made two lengthy trips to New York. When I was there, I missed my family. When I was in Cheyenne, I definitely missed New York.

While attending the Cheyenne schools, I enjoyed learning American history, especially about its heroes such as George Washington, Abe Lincoln, General Grant and the Civil War, etc., but when it came to Buffalo Bill, the Indians, and How the West was Won they seemed to drag things out too much for me. Frontier Days celebration was the biggest event in Cheyenne. That's when its population nearly doubled, and the Mayflower took in thousands daily.

Soon, the days of hot-rodding, dating, and beer drinking arrived. One evening my parents decided to go out to dinner and left me the house so I could invite a few friends over. My guests arrived. After a few boring moments, two of the kids asked me if they could go for a ride by the local drive-ins (the great Owl Inn and the A & W). They explained that they would try and hunt down a few other friends, to liven up our party. I agreed to the idea. Soon, they were back and, to my surprise, it seemed that half of the town's kids around our age had followed them. When I looked outside the whole block had changed. It looked like Hot-Rod City. Our entire house had also changed. It was packed with a whole crowd of teenagers, upstairs, downstairs, and in the back yard. The majority were the town's brightest youngsters.

They had brought several cases of beer, and tons of watermelons. The drinking started and the record player began blasting. The doors were left wide open so everyone could come and go as they pleased. The chief of police lived directly behind our home. I don't believe he heard the racket or that he called his station, but to everyone's surprise the police arrived. Cheyenne's few available police cars made several trips in order to transport my guests and their host to the station. My party, and of course the big beer-bust, made headlines in both of the town's newspapers.

The original idea for the party was my mother's, but the long cleaning job to follow belonged strictly to me. Our entire basement was soaked with melon juice.

During the subsequent court proceedings, I was fined $25 for being the host of a party where beer was unlawfully consumed. Actually, I didn't like to drink, so I never had a drop.

This sort of partying became fashionable with other youngsters. Soon they threw their own parties, and then called the cops on themselves. This way they, too, would become known. (I don't remember any party receiving the publicity mine did, though). At one such party, right after the police arrived I hid in the fire escape with two boys and three girls. Everyone was arrested except us.

Since I had become such a popular figure in the Cheyenne community particularly with the police, it was time to return for another visit to New York. This time, however, it was with my parents' eager approval.

A few days later, I was on my way in my metallic blue hot-rod Oldsmobile with three two-barrel carburetors, chromed engine and wheels, especially built for drag racing. My gas bill broke records. Not the ideal car for New York.

After I had been east only two days—this time in Jersey City— some kids lifted the hood of my car and were looking over the engine. I had just returned from a restaurant with my youngest cousin and his wife. I was dressed in a suit with a white shirt and tie. Concerned with the scene, I ran over to see if my car was okay. That's when two policemen drove up and told everyone to get off the street. All the kids ran away, but I stayed put. Without giving me a chance to explain, two big cops arrested me for disorderly conduct. Early the next morning, Uncle Milton came to my rescue. Again I couldn't help thinking, "What great connections he must have? The best lawyer in town." (The allegations against me were instantly dismissed.)

My residence at the time was in one of Uncle Milton's houses. Neighbors told me that Frank Sinatra had lived close by and, many years ago, Uncle Milton had occasionally treated him to a sandwich and a drink. Uncle Milton also owned a liquor-delicatessen in the area. Many in the store spoke of Sinatra, and some complained that he had never been back to say hello to his old friends. Whenever Uncle Milton was there, he corrected them by explaining that Sinatra had returned several times to see them.

During the evenings, I helped out at a nearby Esso filling station. The old Irishman who owned it was the best boss anyone might choose. There I worked on my car and earned enough money to cover my expenses in New York City. During the weekends I stayed at Uncle Milton's home in Smithtown, Long Island. Uncle Milton and Aunt Helen had gone to Greece for another visit, so I had the responsibility of watching over their properties.

My job at the gas station was only part time, but the experience was invaluable. The Irish boss, Joe (Hood) Finney, had a brother who was an ex-politician. These two brothers shared friends who visited daily and spent much of their time at the gas station.

One was an American-born Italian who had gambled away at the race tracks his share of a furniture warehouse he owned with his brother. Several of the other men were retired businessmen. One of them was a bookmaker, also Italian, who was always available to book bets.

At first, the bookie nicknamed me "Wyoming," until one day when a couple of the men talked me into betting a number in the policy game. Only for fun, I bet a number and some of the men bet along with me. In the evening, after the phone rang to tip us off as to the number that won, the racetrack gambler changed my name to "Pete the Greek", to stay.

"Pete, we won!" Nick Villa, the horse player, yelled out as he stepped out of the indoor wooden phone booth. "Your number was right on the money!"

"We did?" I asked in disbelief, well aware that the odds were stacked against us.

"You did it, Pete!" Matty Burns said with a grin. "The bet pays $540 to each dollar wagered!"

"You broke that damn Black Cat!" Joe Bush said to me smiling, speaking of the bookie.

"Wait a second!" Joe (Hood) Finney, my Irish boss, snapped at the men. "You guys didn't talk Pete into betting the damn numbers racket? You're all in your sixties and some of you are in your seventies.... Pete is only nineteen years old! Whose idea was it to get Pete involved in gambling?"

"I sure didn't have anything to do with it," Big Dutch Charlie answered. "Who's idea was it?"

"I'm totally innocent," John O'Leary commented. "I never gamble."

None of the other men would look at Joe (Hood) Finney after what he said. The gas station owner didn't approve of gambling and lectured the men whenever they brought up the subject.

"Where is that Black Cat?" Bud Finney asked. He was an ex-politician and older brother of Joe Finney. "I can't wait to see the look on his face after you guys break the news to him." He laughed, and then quickly began one of his little tap dances.

"He's across the street at the diner," I answered, a little out of turn but perfectly on time. "He must have gone there to count all his booking action in advance!"

"I don't know about anyone else, but I got him for a bunch of dough," Nick Villa said in an innocent tone and straightened his gray hat, which was pushed far back. "There's that Black Cat....I see him walking out of the diner. He's sure in for a big surprise. He simply can't just walk across the street. First he has to do his usual big show. Look you guys...he's getting into his big Chrysler!"

"I sure hope he doesn't have to hawk it," Matty Burns said.

Once again, all the men laughed. Then no one spoke for the longest time. The men watched the Black Cat start his car and carefully park it on the other side of the street, where the other lot was, which belonged to my boss. Slowly he stepped out of his car. Then, with his head up high and his chest sticking out, he began to walk toward the gas station entrance. Still, nobody spoke as the bookie stepped over the doorsill with his alligator shoes, bringing his bulk into the room. He paced a few steps and took his usual vacant seat near the cigarette machine. Most of the men were standing, but Hood Finney was sitting on his big chair, leaning backwards, with his legs stretched comfortably on his desk.

"Pete the Greek is looking for you, Black Cat," Nick Villa said to the bookie with a serious look on his face.

"Hah, who's that?" the Italian bookie asked, appearing concerned.

"Pete, over there," Nick Villa said, pointing my way.

"Oh...you mean Wyoming." the bookie said, and then looked toward me. "Are you looking for me, Wyoming?"

"How can I be looking for you?" I asked with a grin as I stretched my upper body, flexing my chest beneath a tight T-shirt.

"Well, young man, didn't you just hear Nick say that you're looking all over for me?" said the bookie.

"This is a new one for me," I answered in a serious tone. "How can I be looking all over for you, Black Cat, when I'm staring right at

11

you? Besides, you're never all that hard to find…you're always around to collect your bets."

"Pete the Greek slit your throat," Nick Villa said, attempting to control his laughter. "I certainly hope you turned in all your bets…and didn't book them yourself, Black Cat."

"Did Georgy call in the number?" the bookie asked with the first signs of concern.

"The number came in just the way Pete called it!" Nick Villa quickly answered. "Not bad for a quick pick by a young man from Wyoming…huh Black Cat?"

The bookie didn't say a word. He stood up and walked to the wooden phone booth to call Georgy and double check on the bad news. Meanwhile, the men looked at each other, grinning.

Soon, the bookie stepped out of the phone booth and sat down. His face was now flushed, and perspiration was beginning to show on his forehead.

"In order to pay us all off, you're gonna have to keep paying till hell freezes over…isn't that right, mister Black Cat?" Nick Villa asked.

"Oh, get off it Nick!" the bookie snapped. "You guys broke me! I'm not joking…I'm finished!"

"You were finished long before you ever got started," Nick Villa said, as though he was unloading an old grudge. "We're the ones that made you rich in the first place. Remember those days? But one never knows when a young man may unexpectedly show up from Wyoming and take you for a quick ride straight to the cleaners."

"One never knows anything," said the bookie, and reached for his handkerchief to wipe his forehead.

"How did you come up with that number, Pete?" Joe Finney asked me. "I mean…everyone here should know how you came up with it."

"When Nick asked me to choose a number…the first number that I thought of was the last amount I sold in gasoline," I answered. "And because mister Black Cat always calls me Wyoming…the same number happens to also be my Wyoming license plate number. How's that for simplicity?"

This time all the men laughed, including the Black Cat.

It was getting late, and we had to close the gas station. As each man departed, I was thanked and congratulated for my lucky pick.

The following day the bookie had to go into the bottom of his bankroll to pay everyone off. He also had to increase his income by applying for his two previous jobs, which were promptly given to him starting the very next day. One was at the diner taking cash at lunch, and then in the evening helping out at the gas station.

These men liked me, and I always enjoyed listening to their stories. They spoke a lot about the imprisoned numbers and lottery racketeer, J. V. (Newsboy) Moriarty, how he got arrested and something about a girlfriend turning him in. Also, that $2,400,000 was allegedly found inside a car in a Jersey City garage. Nick Villa explained that he had reason to believe that all the currency was the drop of the week. They also told stories about most of the underground overlords on the East Coast. From the way the stories were told, at times it seemed as if they were best friends with all of them.

Nearly two years later, I left to go back to Denver, where my family had moved. I took fond memories of the East Coast with me. Back in the west, at first I worked in restaurants, but in a short time I was operating one. I enjoyed the nightlife and the flattery I received in this line of business. Those were great years.

My few Greek acquaintances in Denver were also in the restaurant business, and invited me for Poker and Greek Rummy games at the local Greek clubs. These fun games at times turned into pretty heavy action—games like Barbuti, a Greek dice game. Most of the players at these games were respectable individuals. But as in all gambling, among the decent players, there were a few sharpies.

Chapter 2

Fool's Paradise

During the early sixties, the Greek clubs in Denver were protected by private club licenses. The other big games were operated by a group of Italians who also booked track bets, football, and other sports. That's where the real late action took place, which lasted through the next morning and sometimes much longer. At certain moments of the game betting action was high, and the rumors I heard about those games from the older gamblers was that bigger bets were made there than could be made at the tables anywhere in Nevada. What took place in those clubs was always a secret. A secret, however, about which everyone was aware but never discussed.

The stories, which circulated only in confidence, were endless. Some gamblers lost their businesses overnight, and others could not keep up with the high interest charged by loansharks.

Late one night, a private Barbuti game was held at one of Denver's best known restaurants. The final outcome of that game was that the players were held up. The losers were not the ones who lost during the game. The biggest *losers* were the *winners* and big money holders. After they were robbed, they were locked up in the restaurant's walk-in refrigerator. They almost froze to death, till later that morning the chef luckily opened the walk-in door looking for a slab of beef. To his surprise, he found a lot more beef in there than he had stored originally.

Not long after that a game was busted up by the Denver police. It was a game held by a group of Italians, and the bust was the talk of the town for quite some time. Both of Denver's major newspapers printed the facts, and also displayed mug-shots of every player involved.

My father, James, was annoyed and considered it a disgrace to our family that I was attending gambling sessions at the Greek clubs. Therefore, one day he invited me for a serious discussion. At first he began to remind me of a few Greek parables and philosophies. That part was only the warm-up of this conversation. The topic then changed to local underworld gambling (although licensed) versus legal casino gaming operations.

"They are all racketeers with a license!" he cried out. "From the Greek pestholes downtown to the bigger dumps in north Denver. I'm particularly speaking of the sucker trap on the other side of the railroad tracks...right in the heart of Little Italy!"

"How do you know?" I asked in disbelief. "You've never been inside any of those clubs "

"Clubs...?" my father's voice sounded off again, as he burst into laughter and then quickly regained his breath.

"Please, Pete, don't ever let me hear you call them clubs again. Bordellos, just like the ones they call clubs here, have been available in other parts of the world for as long as I can remember. And Pete, you're not the type of person to be keeping company around such corrupt individuals. Besides, you're risking that sooner or later you'll become addicted to gambling."

"I can stop this instant," I laughed. "I'm not hooked. I just play for fun. And I don't care if I never see the sharpies again! But just a second, those sharpies already have some of my money...and I'm going to win it back."

"Some of those half-wits you call sharpies are professional cheats!" James cut me off. "I bet they even auction you off before each game...as to which of them will have the opportunity to cheat you first! I'm referring to their putting you in the middle...for the kill! That's so they can cheat you together! Do you understand what I'm saying?"

"I believe I do understand...but if you know more, please tell me now," I answered impatiently.

"I'm afraid I do know more," he commented, as he paused to collect his thoughts and stood up.

He looked tall and strong as he walked over to the buffet. He opened the cabinet and poured two brandies out of the Metaxa bottle. Then, smiling, he walked back slowly toward me. He placed a glass in front of me and sat in his deep leather chair.

"God forgive me," James started. "For years I've been wishing this day would never come. But here we are, talking about gambling...my long forgotten past."

His eyes looked beyond me toward the lighted chandelier over the table in the dining room. His expression clearly indicated that he was lost in revery about his own past.

It was then that he refreshed my memory of how he had broken the bank more than once at roulette in a resort area not far from Athens called Loutraki.

"Whatever you do, my son, don't go back to those local traps they call coffeehouses or clubs," James said in a serious tone. "I recognized some of the gamblers' mugs in the newspaper. It was embarrassing enough to see that there were some Greeks involved, right next to that group of north Denver Italians and others.... What would you do if they were to get busted for gambling again...and you became one extra face in the newspapers? Soon the restaurant columnists would be writing articles about you...and the restaurant business. You simply can't afford bad publicity. Particularly this type, which will stay on your record forever."

"Yes, father, you're right. I agree," I answered. "But you said you know more. Now please tell me how the sneaky cheats robbed me at cards."

"When you speak of cheats and combine them with gambling, there is no limit as to the methods involved...but I'll try to explain," James answered in disgust. "At Greek Rummy, or Knock Rummy, they use signals and motions to show how many points you're holding in a particular hand. Motions are also used to signal a specific discard the cheat needs...from his friend, the swindler sitting next to him. This goes on and on around the table for hours,

16

leaving you hopeless…with no chance to win!"

"All right, all right!" I cried out. "How, then, since they can't see my cards, do they know how many points I'm holding?"

"There are spectators sitting next to you pretending they're your friends…and many others all around their big games, who are also very curious, are there not?" James asked swiftly, as though he had been there many times to see.

"Yes, but…" I commented, now deep in thought.

"But, nothing!" James said roughly. "Between the cunning cheats and some of the spectators, they'll make a charitable spectacle out of you!"

"I'm getting the urge," I said bitterly, as I stood up and began nervously pacing the floor, thinking of all the incidents I had witnessed that matched every detail of my father's words. "You know, James, I'm getting the feeling that things are going to explode, just like the Fourth of July, at that dump downtown!"

"Such words are not what I would expect to hear from a son I raised with Greek, English, and French schooling," James said. "Besides, those cowards will not fight one by one…gang of wolves that they are."

"It's not just the money." I said in disgust, as I picked up my glass and drank the remaining brandy. "It's the principle…because I trusted them. I've been ripped off, I'm sorry to tell you, for more than ten thousand!"

"Pete, quit now." James said in despair. "That was most of your savings…was it not?"

"Yes, it was." I answered. "That's the reason I want to learn. Don't you see?"

"You're not asking me to teach you how to gamble?" asked my father.

"Yes, I am. And don't worry, I can quit instantly, the day I win my money back."

"Once you learn my son…it's hard to quit. You will only keep on *graduating* to no end."

"You quit…didn't you?"

17

"You've got to be joking. Of course I quit…just before your mother and I were engaged. I was a businessman, not a gambler. To tell you the truth, I never really got started."

"Now I'm convinced that you're joking," I said. "You just told me a while ago that you were the king of the games, that you broke casinos."

"I said no such thing," said my father.

I walked back to my chair and sat down. More childhood memories returned.

"I remember," I said smiling. "We were in Kifisiä when I was around seven years old…at your friend Salvatore's villa. We still have the pictures in our albums. In one picture we're together with mother and the kids…in front of the Packard. There is also another picture of Salvatore's jeep with a soldier chauffeur. There is another picture of a limousine that belonged to those men from the English embassy with whom you played cards."

"You don't forget anything, do you, Pete," my father said. Then, lost in his own thoughts, he smiled and took a generous swallow of his brandy.

"I've got more to tell you." I said. "You gambled against those men from the embassy…and you had more money in front of you than I've ever seen. It was during Greek Halloween. I remember you would secretly hand me your glass of gin and tonic. Then you whispered in my ear, telling me to take your drink out to the garden and water the flowers with it. I must have watered those flowers at least twenty times that evening. You ended up playing cards all night after I went to bed—till the next morning."

"I can't believe you remember all the details," James said with a smile. "You were so young. You know, Pete, we are extremely lucky you and I. Because we do have all those memories. Otherwise, life would be dull."

I promised my father that my visits to the clubs would become less frequent and wider apart. He then explained to me that if I was going to gamble in spite of his warnings against all types of gambling, perhaps someday I should visit Las Vegas. Only once a year maybe, where at least gambling was legal. He suggested that I bet only table minimums and follow his guidelines on the mathematical probabilities.

He emphasized that the games were to be played just for fun, but cautioned me that there would be strict rules to follow. Patiently he explained the fundamentals of games I would be playing in the casinos and defined the terms and slang words and phrases that were common to all types of casino gambling. Then he analyzed for me the differences in the payoffs offered in casinos versus the true odds.

He also showed me the difference between the European Roulette wheel which consists of 36 numbers and a single zero and the American wheel used in Las Vegas, which contains an extra digit, the double-zero.

"The rules and the odds of Roulette in Nevada are different than the European counterpart," James cautioned. "The odds of European roulette are a slim 1.35 percent against the bettor. The Nevada roulette game carries a fearful house edge of 5.26 percent, according to my figures. Therefore, the negative odds grind away against players, for the simple reason that the longer you play the game, the more chance negative odds have to work against you."

"You see," I said, cutting into the flow of my father's words, "I was right. You were the best gambler in Greece. The smartest gambler casino owners had ever seen."

"The only time I was the smartest gambler, Pete, is when I quit gambling altogether," he replied. "This is the best lesson I can ever teach you about all types of gambling. But now that you've been ripped off for ten grand, it's difficult for you to understand that gambling is a vice, even when you gamble among crooks. Knowing that they're dishonest doesn't make any difference, once you're hooked."

"Okay, you're right…but you'll see," I said. "I'll win every dime back. But if they cheat me again…even their father, the devil himself, won't be able to protect them. The one *ruffiano*, who's the Greek kingpin of the bunch, will be the first to 'catch his lunch.' He's the biggest crook of them all."

James exploded in laughter. "Pete, it's okay to joke about those sharpies, but some of them are Greeks. Forget the money you lost and all the grudges or any idea of hostility. That way of thinking is not of Greek culture, remember?"

"All right, but as you explained earlier, I was ripped off...I didn't *lose* the money. Anyhow, I apologize for interrupting you earlier. Please explain how you broke the bank at Roulette. You want me to be smart, don't you? Right now, with the little bit I know about gambling, I feel like a lightweight. I want to be a heavyweight. Is there something wrong with that?"

Calmly, James continued as though he had every word memorized like a poem. He knew all the answers in advance.

"Well, okay, I did win at Roulette," he said. "But only by choosing to lay my money against the odds. That means that I covered the majority of the numbers on the Roulette layout. For instance, I would cover the numbers 1 through 35, leaving the house the 36 and the zero. By doing this, I would *net* one winning unit from my betting action, since the bet pays 35-to-1. When I say betting action I mean the table limit. Sometimes, I would bet even higher if the casino would allow it. The casino had two chances to beat my 35, I figured. However, I wasn't fooled by thinking this type of play would work all the time. Because I knew that the two chances were constantly there, working against me, from the first spin to the thirty-seventh spin. But it made good sense, for the simple reason that it is much easier to choose two numbers out of thirty-seven that would not appear than to try, like most gamblers, to pick one or a few numbers out of 37 that might appear. The single bet I would win, however, was more than enough to cover expenses for a week or longer in Loutraki!"

"How often did you bet this way?" I asked.

"My rule was to give the croupier only one or maybe two chances at the most per day to succeed against me," James smiled. "I would then walk away...and come back periodically, counting only on some inner feeling of good luck."

As our discussion continued we had another brandy, while we

glanced through the pictures in our Greek albums.

Throughout the next few weeks, my father schooled me on statistics and probability. He also instructed me in figuring odds on Craps, Poker, *Chemin de Fer* (Baccarat), and the game *Trianta-ena*, which means thirty-one in English. (Thirty-one was played in Greece and other European countries as commonly as Twenty-one is played in the United States.)

James explained that at the game of Thirty-one the person who is dealing (the Banker) has the edge by far, over all the players betting against him if he takes the action on all bets made. The edge can become even more favorable if the Banker has a choice on *which card* he chooses—out of any cards dealt to his own hand—to *turn up,* as his up-card for the other players to see. An additional edge for the Banker over the player is the rule that the Banker draws last, and can stand at *any count* he chooses.

James also taught me money management, defined the words trend, sequences, progressions, etc., when to start playing, how much to bet, and when to stop.

"Always figure out the odds to the fraction, whether they're in your favor or against you, before you chance a single dollar," he said. "And never forget this one most important rule: when gambling, you're suppose to be going into business, not out of business."

As time passed, fellow Greeks introduced me to other forms of gambling—horse and dog tracks.

A recent police raid at the Barbuti game had effectively brought the local action to a temporary halt. The gang of determined racketeers operating them, however, were not about to give up. They had some of their *ruffianos* spread the word that there were big games held at several locations outside of Denver.

The location of the games changed each evening from one small town to another. This way, no one could be certain where the next game was to be held till the last minute. Every gambler who wanted to see action would have to start by driving to the "gaming headquarters" in north Denver. The time of the gathering was prearranged by phone, and it was usually late at night. From there, the automobile caravan would begin its journey to the specific town in which the game was to take place. The majority of the time, the ride was a lot more distant than a non-gambler would imagine. (A person could easily become extremely healthy, from the fresh air alone, driving those distances). Believe it or not, they held games as far away as Pueblo, Colorado and Cheyenne, Wyoming. Both towns are more than a hundred miles from Denver, one to the south and the other to the north. (Some of the sharpies even purchased maps so they wouldn't get lost.)

They didn't have to await my retaliation for long, though, because I had a plan. I knew, from my little experience at different games, that a gambler under strain or pressure, or feeling any kind of fear, can never win. So one night I escorted them to a Denver hotel only a short distance from the police station. I explained that the hotel was operated by friends. This called for quite a bit of convincing, but I managed to persuade them that the hotel was safe for a Barbuti game. My biggest alibi was the hotel's parking lot. There, their automobiles would not be noticed, as they had been when they were all parked together in front of the north Denver location that was raided by the police.

This time, the caravan of automobiles followed my car to the downtown hotel. I walked in and slipped the front desk manager two folded Benjamin Franklins, just as I had promised him a few days before. He in return handed me the key to a large suite without registering my name.

I informed the sharpies that there was no one registered on that floor, so we had it all to ourselves. Just in case, though, I cautioned them that, since the police station was close by, if the police were to knock, there was one strict rule of which they should be aware. Which was that someone better grab all the dice and flush them down the toilet.

When the Barbuti game started, the sharpies were so frightened that I could barely hear them calling their bets. This was the first time I had ever seen this phenomenon actually work and pay off. Not one of them could throw more than three of four passes in sequence. (It was as if the dice had known.) I began to bet, taking all the side action I could hustle from the non-shooters. The cash was coming my way faster than I had anticipated. Occasionally, when we heard any type of vehicle drive by with a siren on, I would motion for someone to run toward the window to check and make certain it wasn't the police driving up to bust the game.

By daybreak, the sharpies had gone home with empty pockets. All but one of them. He was the self-appointed kingpin of the bunch. He was also the mouthpiece of the north Denver gaming headquarters. He was a Greek who hustled games, booked bets, and had strong-arm connections who loaned money to the players at ten percent a week.

The duel was short indeed. It lasted less than thirty minutes, because, it so happened, I was connecting passes in sequence. After my sixth or seventh pass he refused further action unless I gave him the customary Greek courtesy. Which is, if a player has been extremely lucky and wants the action to continue, he lays odds. Even though Barbuti is a $^{50}/_{50}$ game, I layed 6 to 5, and even as high as 7 to 5, just so I could finish him off and send him off to breakfast, alone. His only company was a $50 bill I gave him, which was the minimum bet.

I was glad I had won, but what thrilled me the most was breaking this minor swindler but big *ruffiano*. This gave me a laugh all the way home—and then some. Because I knew for a fact that the major portion of the money he lost was not his own. It belonged to people who didn't kid around when it came down to collecting money owed to them. These were the operators of the north Denver gaming headquarters.

Chapter 3

The Desert Village

In the summer of 1965, at the age of twenty-two, in a brand new Mustang fastback (and accompanied by my young bride, an attractive young Greek-American named Tricia), I was on my way to my first visit to Las Vegas.

It was the first long trip for the new (but not air-conditioned) automobile. Since the interstate freeway had not yet been built, we drove across the Rockies and then into Salt Lake City and then headed South. Just before leaving Utah, I remember seeing Indian wigwams and a few Mexican shacks. The road through this area was pretty narrow. We had to cut our speed and it felt as though we were driving through a furnace. We passed advertising signs and a few fruit and soft drink stands, and had to stop frequently to permit a brood of chickens to cross the road.

The temperature must have soared past 110 degrees. Red soil all around and the car's heating floorboard indicated our approach to the desert. It was the hottest, dryest climate in which I'd ever travelled.

After speeding up for a few miles we passed a road sign with bullet holes all over it. It said: *Welcome to the State of Nevada—No Speed Limit.*

Since the temperature was rising, the faster I drove the cooler, or should I say the less suffocating, it became. With no speed limit, I was tempted to see what the Mustang could really manage. I pushed it to where I was cruising comfortably at 100 mph.

Soon I noticed that we were gaining on a Corvette. When I finally pulled up next to the 'Vette and was about to pass it, it picked up speed, but so did my Mustang. This nonsense continued as the young guy in the 'Vette was hoping I would run out of gas-pedal. His intentions were not only to win the race, but also to show off to the girl sitting next to him. By now, we were doing over 140 mph and climbing, but who had the time or the nerve to watch the speedometer, since the road was becoming narrower each second. That's about when the guy in the 'Vette finally ran out of pedal. I raced right next to him, fender-to-fender, letting him think the race was a draw. That's when he looked my way and waved. I had only half an inch of gas pedal left, but it was half an inch more than he had. Tricia waved goodbye to our "friends." (Soon we were driving by Nellis Air Force Base, where I was tempted to illegally race a jet fighter which was lifting off. However, Tricia talked me out of that idea.)

Before long, we could see the small town of Las Vegas (around thirty thousand population back then, close to one million presently) as the sun was beginning to fade behind the horizon.

We entered the town from the north side, so we first got a quick look at Glitter Gultch, downtown Las Vegas, and examined the signs and their dazzling lights.

We noticed only a few hotels during our downtown tour. I was beginning to fear that the driving and our entire trip was a waste of time. Since our enthusiasm was diminishing, I turned south, leaving behind what we thought was a disappointing downtown scene.

Shortly, I spotted a tall building with a large neon sign. It was the Sahara hotel and casino, owned by Del Webb at that time. The big hotel appeared luxurious, compared with what we had seen during our quick downtown tour.

"This must be the Strip that I've heard so much about." I said enthused.

"It has to be." Tricia answered. "But whatever it is, it's sure more appealing than those miserable blocks we saw before!"

"That was a small-time carnival scene if I've ever seen one!" I added.

I drove out of the Sahara parking lot and headed up the Strip. There they were, on both sides of the street. Stardust, Desert Inn, Flamingo, Tropicana, and several motel-type casinos. Low in structure, but new and clean looking. I drove up and down the Strip a couple of times, as we looked each of them over because some were designed in Middle Eastern style. Several appealed to us, and we were trying to decide at which hotel we would stay.

"How about the Sahara?" I asked Tricia. "It was the tallest one."

"That would be great," Tricia smiled.

I made a U-turn, and drove there so we could check in and get out of the heat.

As the bellhop escorted us to our room, my mind was on the casino, where all the action was taking place. Soon we entered our room, which was freezing from the cold wind blowing out of the air-conditioner that had been purposely left on.

Tricia unpacked and then drew the curtains open to gaze out the window.

"Pete, look," she said. "There's a big swimming pool out there."

She could no longer see me. I was in the bathroom turning on the shower. Thirty minutes later I was showered, shaved, dressed, and ready for action.

"My goodness," Tricia said. "You just don't know how good the water would feel. I know you're anxious to go down and play, but you could have gone for a swim with me first."

"We have a full week's vacation," I answered. "A person can drown inside that pool in a week's time. That's only if he survives by hiding in the shade, before he burns to a crisp in that desert sun."

"I already know what you're gonna do all week," she cried out. "All you're going to do is gamble!"

"Take your time and do anything your heart desires," I said. "Swim, bathe, and make yourself up. I'll be waiting in the casino. We can play for a while and then have a nice dinner."

"But I'm not old enough to gamble," Tricia complained.

"Don't worry, you look twenty-three." I laughed and hugged her as I headed downstairs.

When I entered the casino area I stopped and watched, standing motionless. While taking in the scene, feeling the magnetic current, I mulled over how I would handle getting my feet wet at the tables.

I better not show my skill right away, I kept thinking. "Just hold back for awhile. I've heard rumors about these people not liking professional gamblers...and they bar the best ones. If I was to show my skill too quickly, they might bar me.

"What if all the players and dealers watched me play? They might learn too much and then break all the casinos...and what would I do then?"

As the employees looked my way occasionally, I suspected they were wondering about my ability to play. I looked back at them, thinking they were a source of money in the bank.

Young rookie that I was, I knew nothing more than the basic fundamentals of the major games. I was totally inexperienced. Even though I was in the middle of the desert, little did I know I was afloat on a deep ocean. (Actually, I was not too far from Death Valley National Monument, otherwise known as Devil's Hole. However, I was not aware of this at the time). I was a real hot shot cavalier, with my personalized graduation papers, which had the usual value of the casino neophyte's opinion of himself.

Suddenly I began to wonder if perhaps I had overdosed with the plush atmosphere, as I tried to snap back into a realistic frame of mind. I began to walk slowly in the direction of the center of the room. The excitement from the noise and very involved gamblers had affected me. Most of the men were wearing suits. The ladies were elegantly garbed in long silk gowns or wore dark cocktail dresses.

At first a busy Craps table drew my attention. It was attended by several players making bets much too fast for me. As I was trying to keep an eye on the action, my instincts told me not to get involved with the game; I simply wasn't ready. They also clearly informed me that once I became involved I would never be the same person ever again.

While I was watching the action, a cocktail waitress asked if I wanted a drink. To show that I knew a thing or two about drinking, I ordered a martini on the rocks. I took a twenty from my pocket to pay for it. Soon, the waitress returned and handed me the drink. I gave her the twenty, and she accepted the bill and thanked me with a curtsy and a big smile. I watched her and my twenty disappear, as she walked around the Craps table serving drinks to the players. Most of the gamblers handed her a chip. One of them, I noticed, didn't even thank her. Two guys, at the other end of the table, got free drinks and cigarettes. I had tipped waiters a twenty before, but for a well served dinner. I had also thrown twenty *single-dollar bills* to belly dancers in New York at the Greek nightclubs. But a twenty for a complimentary drink? Our room for the night was less than that. When she walked by me again, I said, "Miss, I'm ready for my next one, but this time make it straight up...and *skip* the glass. And don't forget to drop two lives inside!"

She laughed at my bartender's expression, and also the fact that I seemed completely unaware as to the fate of my twenty.

Feeling uncertain, I shied away from Craps and Blackjack tables at first. I walked to a Roulette table and bought chips. I was lucky; before long I had my original stack plus some chips of greater value. This lucky streak was repeated several times that night. The croupier's eyes seemed about to jump out of their sockets each time I won a sizeable bet. He couldn't believe it. I just couldn't lose.

We stayed up gambling all night, as Tricia got involved. We won so consistently that several other players placed their chips, following our leads. By daybreak, my pockets and Tricia's purse were loaded with cash and Sahara chips.

The next evening we enjoyed dinner and, since Tricia insisted, we had to sit through a show.

We kept winning in every casino in which we gambled. (This stunning good luck is what made me become the believer I am today in beginners' luck.) When we returned to Denver, my winning memories and the taste of the Las Vegas atmosphere were deeply implanted. I thought of Las Vegas constantly, foreseeing a promising future at this new wonderland.

On the following trip, I wasn't as lucky at Roulette, so I ignored the game completely. (That was the starting point and the inauguration of my understanding of the difference between lucky and unlucky streaks). Instead I moved to the dice pit. I was betting the Pass Line and placing the numbers, 4, 5, 6, 8, 9, 10—following the usual procedure of nearly all other Craps-shooters.

On future trips, after extended mathematical figuring and experiments with dice and cards, I picked up more skillful gambling techniques. I could finally attack the Blackjack tables with confidence. Also, with the help of an encouraging winning streak, I built up my stake playing Craps, as I switched to the Don't Pass and Don't Come. From then onward I played those two games successfully, winning on most of my trips. I was under the impression that winning at table games was simple. The most difficult task to overcome was the enormous discipline required for successful money management. My major losses occurred when I overlooked the persistence of stubborn losing streaks and remained at the same table to ride out losing sequences. Following a few hazardous losses, I became wiser, and ignored tables where I could not win quickly. I realized that only winning was fun! Losing was for losers—and for the casinos I frequented. The evidence of my successful efforts was an enlarged gambling stake.

When I gambled in Denver, I played Poker and Barbuti at the local clubs. The games were operating again with a private club license. My disposition to activate my increased knowledge proved hazardous as I depleted the sharpies' featherweight bankrolls. Of course, none of them liked me much anymore, but I had gained their respect. Each time I exhausted their resources I returned to Las Vegas.

Las Vegas was beginning its rapid growth. Hotels were being rebuilt with highrise towers. The Sands already stood high, and Caesars Palace was being built from the ground up. The latter opened in August of 1966.

In 1967, Howard Hughes began negotiations to purchase several casinos. His first major Las Vegas transaction was the acquisition of the Desert Inn at a cost of $13,000,000. Then he applied for a license to operate the Castaway Casino. His next essay was the Frontier Casino. In 1968, he attempted to purchase the Stardust Hotel and Casino, but the billionaire's plan was thwarted. He did acquire the off-the-beaten-track Landmark. (By the time Hughes vanished from his Desert Inn suite in 1970 he owned seven major Nevada casinos.)

Then, a short distance away from the Strip, the International Hotel (not yet operating with the Hilton name) was being built. This huge structure of more than 1,500 rooms opened in 1969 and was the largest hotel in the world.

The expansions, along with the public's insatiable demand for casino gambling, brought greater and greater crowds to the former desert village. Along with growth came more prostitution, drugs, crime, and hustling of every type. But the city responded with one of the best organized and efficient police forces in the country.

A small group of casino hustlers made a living by delivering names of various high rollers to various casinos and, in payment, receiving as much as three percent of a player's losses. (This situation continues today.)

I stayed in Las Vegas several weeks at a time on my visits. Most of the time I kept an eye on the Craps tables, waiting for streaks. I ground out losing streaks with minimum action until my kind of streak appeared. And sooner or later the dice ran "cold," allowing me to perform at my usual high-rolling pace.

I tried to be a smart young gambler, carefully enforcing money management rules and procedures. Drinking at the tables was a no-no. After I became known in most casinos, envy of my knowledge of the games and my self control was obvious on the faces of some dealers and pit bosses. I was recognized in each hotel when I walked through the door. Casino managers, however, were always glad to see me, and their hands eagerly reached out in greeting. I always left big tips behind each time I scored. There were times I tipped generously even when I lost. My room, food, and beverage costs were picked up by the house. I was asked to stay as long as I wanted by the casino managers. They wanted players, especially if they were high rollers, and it didn't matter if they won occasionally. The various casino executives were well aware that it was the big gamblers who attracted all the small-time action—the everyday tourists who, frequently, departed from Las Vegas penniless.

In time, I met players from all over the United States as well as from countries around the globe. Some of them strayed for only a brief period. When they did come back, weeks or months later, they would bring a brand new bankroll which in time was dispersed. In most cases, the only reward the bettors got in return for their losses was the good time they experienced during the short period their stakes lasted. The ones who visited the town often were glad to find me there, still winning. When players whom I knew well were major losers and were in need of money, they almost always received a loan from me. (Those were the days when a gambler's word and a handshake were sufficient bond.)

During that era, casino executives offered loans to high rollers without the borrower having to fill out lengthy credit forms.

This gracious eleemosynary support didn't last forever, though. With regret, I witnessed this system, just like most things in life, come to a conclusion.

The obvious reason was abuse—and too much of it. Some casino pit bosses, as well as players, took advantage of the system in ways which displayed nothing but greed. Some players borrowed money which was never paid back. A sidebar of this issue was that some shift bosses—without knowing the borrowers' real intentions—even loaned money to artistic deadbeats. These swindlers had little or no intention of returning to that casino, or even to Las Vegas, depending on the size of the loan and management changes in that casino. Also some pit bosses regularly comped an assortment of personal friends who rarely gambled.

After all this, management got the word from the top to cut down on practically everything. The operating methods were quickly modified.

As the sixties became history, I observed the continuing changes in casino operations. The changes applied to the rules of the table games, new minimum and maximum wagering bases, management, and, most particularly, the ownership of individual casinos. The time had come for what Wall Street called the "corporate" era. The era of alleged underworld control was headed for limbo.

Pit bosses had to keep track of a customer's play—the size of his wagers as well as his playing time at a given table. This applied in particular to comped players. They also had to keep accurate records of chips delivered as well as the players' cash before it was dropped into the lock box beneath the tables. There were other changes which were strictly enforced.

It seemed that there were new regulations in play on each of my subsequent Las Vegas trips. Even the game of Blackjack varied among casinos. How many decks were to be used in a shoe, whether the player's cards were dealt face up or down, or one up and one down—even new ways of shuffling were taught to dealers. All of these modifications led to increased house profits.

Formerly, chips of a specific casino were accepted at all other casinos, either for redemption or table play. Losers might sign markers at one casino and take the chips elsewhere for redemption. The new regulations made the chips redeemable only at the casino of origin. There had been rumors of counterfeiting.

About the same period, many of the "boys" who ran things for what some called "The Mob" began to retaliate. They complained that their positions were being filled by new, casino-law-abiding extremists who operated according to the new rules of the computer era, and who were skeptical about comping even a meal ticket without first calculating the play. The old boys didn't approve of the new regulations, since they threatened to take away their control of the action. Thus, big decisions were arrived at which made perfect sense to some of the old scientific swindlers in some of the casinos, one of which could have taken in the public with perhaps the most devious hustle known in the annals of dice games. I call this method *The Hypothetical Setup,* since it has more than logic behind it. I was told by a veteran gambler that the scheme originated in the prohibition era, when cheating with dice was pretty advanced.

(Incidentally, I made money each time I took advantage of this swindle.)

The way this hypothetical setup is executed is that before the dice are returned to the shooter they are turned over by the stickman consistently to the same number as the shooter's point on the Pass Line. Since the shooter and most side players bet on the Pass Line, the results of this play didn't remain a mystery for too long to my young mind, which was eager to learn. (I'll be the first to admit that this method of flipping the dice does not always work against the shooter's Pass Line point. But if it is done consistently, it can throw off the succession of winning sequences. I must also explain that not all casinos were working this setup. Only certain casinos used it consistently. The real truth will only surface after millions of players who have witnessed the flipping of the dice through the years become aware of the purpose and then think back, recalling each incident and where it took place.)

When questioned as to why they flipped the dice to the shooters point, the stickmen said that it pleased their customers, and made them feel lucky. Thus, no one knew the real truth, and the theory remained a secret. Each time I heard this explanation, I shook my head emphatically, but sadly. (The players who have noticed this turning of the dice throughout the years, and have lost big money because of the manipulation, may write to me through the publisher of this book.)

Sure, it was sometimes easier for me to win by betting on the Don't Pass. Particularly when I had the help of the stick-working wonders on the Don't side of the table. However, I felt guilty every time. So I played a major role in spreading the word around, making sure to alert players of the details of this flipping procedure.

"Don't ever throw the dice the way they're brought to you, after they've been flipped to your point," was my advice. I was aware, however, that by emphasizing this I could be endangering my winnings.

The worst part of the setup is that it took several years and complaints from the public before anything was done about it. (In fact, it has been used against me in more recent years when betting on the Don't side, in a different way. I will explain in a later chapter.)

The more I gambled in Las Vegas, the more I was beginning to understand several other dubious methods endorsed by certain casinos. At the same time, I couldn't help discovering a great deal about the other players who shared the tables with me as I watched their chips dwindle. The majority of bettors appeared as if they had patterned their games by watching others and then betting the same way. Many of them had even misnamed the game, calling the game "Seven Eleven." These were the type of people who also advised other players how to gamble without having a clue about the odds of the game they were explaining. They made up stories explaining how much money they won once after betting a particular way. It seemed as if each of them had his own special losing formula to teach others (as long as someone would listen and believe such nonsense), his personal system, based on his own supposed expertise. Of course, this always turned out to be expensive for the party who was doing the listening.

The word "Craps" translates as "Hazard" in French. Therefore, anyone who would play a game with this name should know all the angles and proceed with caution.

I was aware that if I continued to gamble in Las Vegas I would always face a *minus odds expectancy* on each table. On the other hand, I also understood that casinos had one big weakness, which was the house limit. Casino operators always had to book my action up to the table limit. I had plenty of experience from private games to know that my most effective weapon, when attempting to break my opponents, was my *money management skill*. Which means that I would never give the other players any sizable action *when they were winning*. At the same time, I also understood how difficult it was to get all the action I needed *when I was winning*. This was always my biggest advantage over the casino industry.

My gambling stake fluctuated, although I greeted winnings and the many frustrating losses with an indifference puzzling to other players. My attitude towards money and my willingness to take high risks impressed some of the toughest players around.

During this time, I met an assortment of high rollers, including several underground overlords. The playing fields moved from New York to Chicago and most of California.

My ability to perform accurately under the constant pressure provided by high stake gambling prevailed against opponents. Predictably, my opponents believed that my lopsided winnings were the results of astronomical amounts of good luck.

My visits to Denver were frequent because of my family and various business matters, that had to be taken care of. While in Denver, I occasionally dropped in at the local games, where I gambled against several of my old acquaintances. Some of them were the usual sharpies, the cunning cheats who put faith in their ability to manipulate cards or dice. A few of these swindlers held private games and invited the usual players, who were ripped off quite regularly. At these games, more than once, the dice were loaded and the cards were marked. I tried to treat these people with compassion, even lending them money when they were tapped out. My largesse even extended to bookmakers who were relieved of their horseroom profits. Some of these guys could not understand an act of friendship, so I felt it an obligation to use my skills to teach them many a costly lesson.

Chapter 4

Bucking the Odds

Feeling the need for a vacation from Las Vegas, I decided to drive to St. Louis to visit a friend. He was a young plunger who invested in thoroughbreds, hoping to hit a jackpot in that business. Ari had been calling me for several months, and when I showed up he welcomed me with graciousness. For several days I couldn't pick up a tab. Everything was prepaid in advance by Ari. During my stay, we visited the racetrack daily. Afterwards, if there were no Greek Barbuti games available, we spent our evenings at the best restaurants and nightclubs in St. Louis. During the period when Ari and I were gambling friends, I saved him a great deal of money and once rescued him from a minor, but what could have been catastrophic, defeat.

In 1970 at a New York poker game, Ari had gone broke. After lending him a fresh bankroll, I watched as he began to recover most of his losses. Meanwhile, though, he was drawn into an argument with several other players. Luckily for Ari, I acted as the referee and straightened out the dispute.

Another time in St. Louis, as we ordered dinner Ari became involved in a Barbuti game with the restaurant's owner. Ari lost $10,000 before dinner was served. I loaned him $2,000 and he won back his loss, plus $3,000 profit, long before our well-done lamb chops arrived at the table.

Once, much later in Chicago during a stormy winter, it snowed so heavily that the racetrack closed down. With no racing, the two horses Ari owned had to stay in the barn. Irked by not prospering from the money he might have won if his animals had run (not to mention a not inconsiderable share of the purses), he invited some friends to our hotel suite for a "friendly" but high-stakes game. While awaiting the other players to arrive, Ari challenged me to play him Blackjack head-on and suggested we play for $100 a hand. I countered that we were friends and were merely killing time. After further convincing, he agreed to drop the bets all the way down to twenty-five cents.

As the game progressed, I noticed that both Ari and his trainer doubled each time one twenty-five-cent wager was lost. In less than an hour the trainer quit and my friend was down close to $5,000. When the game broke up I offered Ari the return of most of his losses. With his pride intact, he refused my offer, so we settled by my undertaking all the expenses for the time we were in Chicago.

During my brief visit in St. Louis I noticed that Ari's gambling methods had not changed. He was the same impatient bettor with the same reckless disregard for the various rules. To this day he remains a high roller and a man of integrity. Fortunately, he is a very good handicapper.

After a few days I drove to New York City for a two-month gambling foray. I phoned old acquaintances (and fellow plungers) who invited me to various Greek and Italian games and some sponsored by an Irish group. These high-stakes games were always on the level, with much higher action than at Vegas. After a few weeks of highrolling with some of the nation's most honest heavy hitters, I knew I had the bug, and was beginning to wonder whether I would ever shake this fever.

The next evening I departed for Chicago, drove all night, through most of the next day, and found an old gambling friend at Arlington Park by the paddock area that afternoon. He had just won on a Kentucky horse, called Lotta Botta. The horse was a long shot, which was part of a $370 Exacta. I was only moments late for that race. The old gambler, though, was right on the money with tickets to win, Quinellas and Exactas. Later that day, he liked another Kentucky horse, owned and trained by the same stable as Lotta

Botta. The horse was called Greek Fortune. The old man and I bet a bundle on that race to win, to place, and on Exactas. We contributed towards making that horse the favorite of that race, as the odds dropped down. The gallop was no real contest for Greek Fortune. He took the race easily, from the stretch all the way to the wire. The payoff wasn't that great, but after the misfortune in New York, the Greek Fortune win was sweet sugar cubes indeed.

For several days in Chicago, I was handicapping my own horses, winning on some and mostly losing on others. One day, at the racetrack, the old gambler and I were invited to one of the biggest private games in the Windy City.

We drove to the meeting location, which was a large apartment building on Lakeshore Drive. All the invited guests were present early, anxious to depart for the big game. From there, two limousines picked us up for a short drive to the Marina area, where we all boarded a good size yacht. The boat departed and headed East towards the Indiana border.

During this time the necessary introductions were made by the host of the gaming operation—which was a floating game indeed. Drinks, various snacks, cigarettes, and cigars were offered to everyone on board by two smiling fun-girls wearing brief tops, mini skirts and high heels.

The old gambler introduced me to several of his friends, who were local Chicago businessmen. Some of them were from the Chicago Loop area. Another man was from Melrose Park—and two others, who were closer to the host, were from Cicero.

The main room of the boat had two Poker tables and a pool table where the Craps was to be held. (It's obviously difficult for anyone's mind to imagine that people can actually play pool onboard the unbalanced surface of a floating boat. But for good reason, such was the case on this boat—as six playing cards were layed out face up on the pool table). When I walked over to take a good look at the Craps arrangement on the pool table, I quickly figured that the playing cards were the numbers 4, 5, 6, 8, 9, 10 which are the six, of any numbers, a Craps better may have as a point. (This was, if the Coast

Guard or any other unexpected problem suddenly arose, all the gamblers had to do was sit at the Poker tables and pretend they were playing Bridge, for match-sticks.)

The boat anchored, but we did not know the exact location. All the men aboard walked to their preferred gambling spot, surrounding the pool table. The old gambler and I were the final players to join the game. After a few minutes of chatter, each of the players reached for his bankroll and the game began.

Throughout the evening I bet low when the dice were passing, but when they ran cold, my action hiked up to the peak allowance. The old gambler followed my betting method, which was to wager on the Don't Pass against every Pass.

By the early morning hours, most of our opponents had gone bust—as their bankrolls had been scattered to other directions. The new legatees and controllers of their loot were the game's host, his two friends from Cicero, the old gambler, and myself, of course.

Since the action at Craps had diminished, the host suggested that we play Poker—as he was anxious to sweep up the entire balance of remaining greenbacks.

For the next few hours, five of us played Seven Card Stud. We were watched by several spectators. In the meantime, the fun-gals were always around for drinks, snacks, and taking a good dose of teasing remarks. During this period, the host and his two friends from Cicero played cautiously. The old gambler and I also used our own techniques and money management.

At one point, the host won a pot with a full house, which totaled close to $20,000. Most of us contributed toward the buildup of that particular pot. As the game continued, each player was desperately attempting to recoup his losses by drawing the host into the hand. He, though, folded most cards, waiting for something good to be dealt his way, and sucker the others in another big pot. Nearly an hour passed by without a big pot. That's when the host accused everyone of playing too conservatively. Most of the players laughed at him for playing the same way. At that point, I teased him for being extremely cautious, hoping to change his strategy and draw him into a big pot.

39

"Are you playing shotgun-style, mister host?" I asked. "Must you have three of a kind before you play out a hand?"

"You're much younger than everyone else here, Pete, so stay out of the conversation and mind your own business!" he answered. "Besides, if you need to learn anything about gambling, just ask the man who's made millions gambling...me!"

"Pardon me, sir, perhaps you're right," I teased. "Maybe you did win enough all night to go into an early, long, wealthy retirement."

Every man in the room began to laugh at my quip.

"What an amusing sense of humor," said the host. "You guys want action? I'll give you action. It's almost noon, and we'll have to head back soon, regardless. From now on, the opening bet goes up to fifty dollars—no more twenties. Can everyone here live with a fifty dollar ante?"

Every man agreed to raise the ante. I said nothing.

"Is fifty bucks too much for you, Mister Greek?" the game host asked.

"Don't rule me out of this game just yet," I answered. "If it's okay with everyone here, let's make things really interesting. We'll hike up the ante to a hundred—and no smaller bet than a hundred will be made during this game. This way, we can all play shotgun style."

Everyone laughed, as each player glanced at one another and then agreed on this rule.

Several hands later, after the cards were dealt, the host had a King showing, as he glanced at his two face-down cards. He then threw an additional $100 in the pot as his opening bet. The next player in line was my friend, the old gambler, who tossed his cards in. I was dealt a Queen up with two Aces as my down-cards. After a few moments of hesitation, I called his $100 bet and raised him $200. The players to my left were the two men from Cicero, and they folded their hands. The host peeked, once again, at his down-cards. He then called my $200 and raised me $500. I, in return, called his $500 and raised him another $1,000. This time his bet was $2,000, and I only called the extra $1,000 worrying about three kings. The next cards were the deuce of clubs to the host, and the Ace of diamonds to me. Now, I had become the high man with the Ace, but I patted my hand on the table, checking to the host. (The purpose for checking my hand was to lead my opponent to believe I was building a straight, since I had an Ace, Queen showing. In addition, I didn't want him to think I had three of a kind.)

"What's wrong, Pete?" the host asked. "All of a sudden you got cold feet?"

This remark resulted in snickering from several spectators, but the players at the table remained quiet.

"My entire body is quite warm, thank you!" I assured him.

The King bets a thousand," the game host said proudly, and threw ten Bengies in the pot.

"That's great," I answered, appearing nervous. "But now you must excuse me while I calculate the potential of my Ace Queen."

After examining my down-cards, pretending I was comparing their value with the Ace, Queen already exposed, I called his $1,000 and raised him $5,000. The host lifted a fistful of Benjies, anxious to raise again, but then changed his mind and only called my $5,000 bet. The man from Cicero dealt out the next two cards. This time he reached for his down-cards and glanced at them for a period, which to me, seemed infinite.

"Two little deuces bet five little thousand," he said with an ironic smile. "Try matching this bet, Mister Greek!"

A few of the spectators laughed at this new crack. The men at the table remained somber and silent. My friend the old gambler was looking in my direction with a gloomy expression.

Figuring that the host had filled up with three Kings and two deuces, I now had to call the $5,000.

"Earlier, you said I had cold feet," I commented in a tone of frustration, and pushed the five grand in the pot. "Well, yachtman, your two little deuces just amputated both of them."

"How can you call my bet with a broken straight?" the game host asked, obviously toying with me. "I've got the King you're looking for over here—can't you see?"

Well aware that he was attempting to irritate me into losing my control, so he could set me up for the kill, I said nothing. the next cards were dealt. He received an eight—no value. My card was a 10, thus giving me a two-way hand. (Any Queen, Jack or 10 would result in a full house. A King would fill-in for an inside straight. But that was an unlikely expectation, because the game host had to be betting his money on a few Kings to begin with. Plus, no straight was gonna win that pot. The odds were stacked no matter how I figured the situation.) His next bet was $5,000 which told me that he had a full house.

However, I had no choice, since I had been in similar situations many times before. It was difficult to hide my emotions, but I reached for the cash and called the bet. He was studying my motions like a old watchdog, as he appeared pleased that I called the five grand.

"Hold the deal for a minute," the host said. "I'm a merciful man, and I want to prove this to you, Pete. I'll give you the opportunity to drag back your last five thousand if you fold your cards right now and surrender to my two little deuces."

Most of the spectators laughed, and then the room became silent. The only sounds heard were the waves splashing on the sides of the boat. Every man watching the game awaited my response. Our host was now in total control anticipating my folding.

I finally answered: "Why don't you can all that mercy and let the man deal the next two cards?"

The next two cards were our last, and were dealt face-down. As usual, I didn't touch my card 'til my opponent first had a good look at his own card. He took his time looking at all his down-cards and studied my apathy. Then, he pushed the remainder of his stake to the center of the table. I felt my heart beating rapidly and felt blood rushing to my face, as I glanced at my own cards. It was the Queen of hearts that flashed brilliantly, which gave me Aces full of two beautiful Queens. My eyes rose instantly to stare at the host, who was sitting across from me smiling. I didn't believe he had four Kings.

"How much are you betting?" I asked him, looking directly into his eyes.

His relaxed attitude changed to an expression filled with panic. As he counted the money, everyone in the room remained silent.

"It's forty-eight thousand, five hundred dollars," he muttered in a low voice. "You don't have to call all of it, Pete, if you don't want to."

"There is one certainty about gambling," I answered with great emphasis. "Once a decision has been made, it's too late to reverse it by changing your mind."

The onlookers held their breath. I counted the money, matching his final bet. No sooner than I finished pushing the cash in the pot he picked up his down-cards and turned them over.

"There you are...three Kings full with deuces!" he said. "Can you beat them or not?"

"I'm gonna have to disappoint you," I murmured, and turned over my own full house. "Three Aces and two gorgeous little girls!"

The applause which followed is still remembered. I pulled all the money in front of me, and stood to stretch my arms to release some of the tension. I thanked our host for the elegant hospitality he provided. The game was now over, and most of the cash was on my side of the table.

When we returned to Chicago, the old gambler headed straight for his hotel, where he could seek plenty of sleep. When I entered my room, I tried to rest, but I was so stimulated that sleep was impossible.

Chapter 5

Monastic Winner

Soon, my visits to Las Vegas began again. I was consistently bringing back large sums of money. My intention was to constantly improve my gambling capabilities and techniques by picking up new winning methods as I examined my mistakes of certain past performances.

The foremost clue to success at casino gambling is to play and win at a game where the house odds are at their lowest. Then, strict money management rules are the key, which almost always provide sizable profits. My strategy always remains the same, which is to win many small battles and, once I have built up a large stake, bet a big portion of it on a single event. Most commonly, I bet the bankroll on a sporting event, attempting to double the bundle on a single wager.

During my early gambling career at Las Vegas, most of California, the Mideastern states, and all over the East Coast, many heavy hitters crossed my path. Some of these high rollers were high ranking mob figures. Each time I gambled against one of them at poker or craps and left him surprised by my play, I experienced the satisfaction of being something of a young legend.

Up or down, but never short on self-esteem, always well dressed, I frequented the nation's best hotels, country clubs, and restaurants. I was free with the greenbacks, spreading more of them among others than for my own personal needs. Everywhere I traveled, I made sure I left some individuals indebted to me, regardless of whether or not they were in need of money. I never borrowed money from any gambler (this stands true to this very day), but I always owned lopsided numbers of bad debts.

I was certainly no fool, but there were plenty of artful swindles awaiting my discovery. With growing maturity, I realized that the experience of losing hung over the heads of most gamblers like a dark cloud. There was more than one sad story behind every flashy exterior. The fates against them were not always self-created. For that reason, I felt compassion for them. Hopefully, they will finally find the light at the end of their long, dark, and complex tunnel. Many players are gambling addicts, without knowing the meaning behind the word. It is my fervent hope that some of the material in this book will help them when their money is at risk. Of course, they can always have recourse to Gamblers Anonymous, but that is a path few addicts enjoy trodding. If they continue to play, let them protect themselves with some of my systems.

Successful gambling consists of diligent money management, superior knowledge of the games, immense patience, and monastic self-control. A gambler must have definite plans concerning both private and casino gambling. He must also possess the know-how, which unfortunately comes only after many years of experience, to handle all situations. Consistent winners at casino games are rare, since winning the majority of bets at the minus odds expectancy is the toughest task in gambling.

It was during the 1970s when I awakened one evening at a Las Vegas hotel. I reached for my watch and noticed that I had been asleep for nearly fourteen hours. It was now 7:00 P.M. For the previous five days in a row I had stayed up gambling. I had played Craps, Blackjack, and Baccarat, and lost consistently. Obsessed with losing, I had broken my most important rule, which is never to chase fortune when it runs from you. Despite all efforts, I had dropped $20,000.

Unable to win, but still armed with $30,000 I decided to decrease my betting to the house minimum until luck changed. It so happened that on that night half the Strip was experiencing a blackout. Business, though, was normal, since casinos have their own generators to prevent looting and to keep the action going.

Since the rule at the casino I was playing at was to change cards hourly at all single deck tables, I noticed the pit boss placing a new deck at a Blackjack table. The farthest seat to the right of the dealer was vacant. From that seat I would be able to count more cards, prior to making any decisions on my own hand.

Without hesitating I took the seat and bought $20 worth of chips. Somewhat humiliated because the high roller of the previous five days was going to bet deuces ($2 per bet), I made my first wager. The look I received from the lady dealer showed compassion (although feeling of this nature is quite rare in Las Vegas) as she shuffled the new deck. She was aware that I had been up several days, and was chasing a losing streak. (Throughout the five-day marathon, I had one bowl of soup each day, bottled water, and lots of orange juice for sustenance. I was alert, however, as I prepared to play the game properly, in case a winning streak developed.)

I hit a Blackjack on my first hand. A quick hint of a grin crossed my face, as I thought, "Look at this hand…and I'm only betting two bucks." On impulse, I pressed my bet to $5. My next hand was also a winner. I let the $10 ride. The next winning hand brought me $20. I let it ride once again and won. This time I pulled back $20 and bet $20 on the next. To my satisfaction I again won. A $40 bet was the logical bet to pursue. I won three more hands at $40. After the next three wins I pressed my bet to $160, and stayed at that level for five more winning hands. Then the streak ended. I tried two more hands at $10 and lost them both. I toked the dealer, stood up, and walked straight to a Craps table.

I bet $5 on the Don't Pass. The first roll was *ace-deuce*, so I pressed the bet to $10. Then the shooter rolled a 9. I laid $30 against the 9. The shooter soon sevened. I bet $60 on the Don't Pass. The next point was 10. I laid $120 against it, since it was a double odds table. The shooter sevened again. This time the dice came around to me. I motioned to the stickman to pass me up because I figured the dice were running cold enough. (I should explain that a shooter can actually shoot the dice even though he is betting on the Don't Pass. He may also change the dice at any point in the game.) The two die-hard shooters who remained at that table were very unlucky. By the time the trend ended, I was ahead over $1,500 at Craps alone.

46

When I walked to the cashier's cage to cash around $2,300, the lights came back on. Along with that pleasant surprise, the lights turned on in my mind. For the first time in five days, I could see clearly. (A player's vision clouds when undergoing a prolonged losing streak.) As I counted the money I felt pretty good. I was aware that the average gambler, with two winning streaks as I had and starting with a $2 bet, would have walked away with perhaps a $100 profit. He or she would have been afraid to back up the two winning streaks, by plunging into deeper waters with bigger bets. It was now time to stoke myself. I walked to the bar, had a double cognac, and headed straight to my room. (That was the first and only drink I had throughout the five days and nights I had gambled.) When I entered my room I bathed, sipping my cognac. I wanted to continue for one more day. When I hit the bed I slept for the rest of the day.

In the early evening when I awoke I was well rested. After I showered and dressed, I was anxious to leave the room. Once I got to the main level, I walked through the hotel's lobby, bypassing the casino. At the front entrance I caught a cab. Despite the fact I was comped, I asked the driver to take me to a restaurant away from the strip. I wanted to forget about gambling, forget that I was even in Las Vegas. I needed that period of contemplation so I could make a fresh start. (A gambler must have confidence that he will win, or he stands little chance at the tables.) The cab driver said that he knew of a very good restaurant on Sahara Boulevard. I killed nearly two hours there. I had pleasant conversations with the staff, which was helpful in establishing the emotional calm required before taking on the tables again. Soon, I felt I was ready.

From the restaurant I cabbed back to my Strip hotel. There, I played $5 Blackjack to test my luck. As soon as I was sure that I was on a winning streak, I hiked my wagers to a more realistic level, and I began to bet black chips.

I played through the evening into the morning hours. Without experiencing a significant winning streak, the $2,300 I won the previous morning had grown to $5,500 by the time I packed it in. In the morning, I chased a winning streak at another hotel, and won at most of the tables.

My playing plan consisted of money management techniques that had been tested for several years, succeeding as long as winning streaks appeared during any playing period. I would begin the play with a $25 bet if I was at a Blackjack game, and $25 plus lay double odds at Craps. If I lost a total of ten units I would leave that table. But if I won from the start, I would double the amount of the bet. If I lost a single bet I would drop my bet to the original $25 I had set as my standard bet prior to the play. If I happened to lose at three different tables, my $25 bets would drop to $10 or even $5, till I built up my stake to where it was at the beginning. After this I would go right back to $25 betting. But when I won a few thousand, I built my minimum bet to $50 per hand at Blackjack, and $50 plus the odds I layed at Craps. If I won a few more thousand, I would build my minimum bet to $100 and then go up as I won. In other words, I would grade winnings and various losses according to the size of my stake, and by the results of wins and losses. I didn't bet wildly. One thing for certain, when the dice or cards began to fall against my bets, I would stop gambling altogether for that day.

I didn't always follow my money management method, as I proved when I stayed up five days losing. Almost every time I broke my rules, the results were disappointing indeed. My rule was to stay up more than a full day to gamble when I was winning. Thus, I was taking full advantage of winning streaks among the various tables, acquiring chips of higher value. It's very simple to understand the fact that when a gambler wins a thousand bets at $50, the total he has won is $50,000. Let's assume that during that same period he also lost eleven hundred bets at $25. That equals $27,500. If we now deduct his total loss from his win, he's $22,500 ahead, regardless of the fact that he lost a hundred more bets than he won. No professional gambler bets the same amount all the time, especially at a minus odds expectancy, because the ultimate result will be minus indeed. The fluctuating structure of a player's wagers is the only successful strategy known and is practiced by the experienced gambler. It makes no difference whether a player is young, old, professional, or new at the tables as long as he follows money management rules and increases and decreases his wagers at the proper time. This rule holds true only in the long run, however, and cannot be considered a winning formula for a few minutes of play. The more increasing and decreasing you juggle, the more profit you will net in the long haul. Luck, in card or dice games, comes in three different categories: good, bad, and what casino habituates call choppy.

Again, when luck runs good, you must bet higher. When luck runs bad you must decrease the size of your bets considerably or stop altogether. But when it runs choppy—which means the wins and losses are equally matched in value with no winning sequences in between—that's when the house has an edge in all wagers, even when the money management method is used. Such choppy tables are to be avoided in the same manner as unlucky tables.

While I kept winning more than I was losing, I was following all types of money management procedures. Without doubt, I was becoming very popular with the pit bosses of each pit. The shift boss, whom I had never met before, also appeared extremely curious.

I was at a Craps table, making sizable bets on the Don't Pass and Don't Come, when the shift boss (who was new) walked up to me.

"I hear you're Greek...are you?" he asked.

I had been expecting this distraction since I was winning and my concentration and momentum could use a little distraction to slow me down, according to his viewpoint.

"Am I winning?" I countered.

"Oh, you seem to be doing fairly well," he said.

I stayed at that table and won throughout the afternoon. By then, the $5,500 had grown to $20,000. At the same casino, I walked to a player-free Blackjack table. My first bets were $25 per hand and they stayed at this level because there was no obvious winning trend. After several hands the cards did what they usually do, if a player is patient. They began to fall my way. After the fourth win I pressed and doubled my bets accordingly. Before long, I was close to $1,000 ahead and again got the same shift boss's attention. Smiling, he walked up to the Blackjack table bringing with him a brand new deck. My dealer turned and whispered to him that I was a professional. The shift boss nodded his head. Even though the dealer was now dealing out of a new deck, I continued to win, building up my bets to the house limit.

Shortly I had a new dealer, and dropped my bets back down to $25. The cards began to fall in my favor, and again I had a new deck. In less than five minutes the shift boss brought yet another new deck. The latest deck wasn't as kind, so I quit and went to cash in at the cage. As the cashier counted my chips, she asked if I had any markers out. (A marker is a voucher a gambler signs to withdraw chips at any gaming table, either on prearranged credit or cash previously deposited at the cashier's cage.) I told her to ask her boss, who was a few feet behind her holding several large yellow envelopes. When she attracted his attention he put down the load from his hands and walked in my direction.

"Hi ya," he said with a smile and shook my hand. "Where have you been? I haven't seen you for some time!"

"I was only here a few nights ago and dropped ten big ones," I answered. "But when I'm up late losing you're in bed sleeping. I wish I could make the kind of money you do when I'm asleep."

"Looks like you won it all back today with interest," he laughed. He glanced at the currency being counted by the cashier. "You're not leaving...are you?"

"I was about to," I answered, pocketed the cash, and left that casino.

My new choice was a long forgotten casino in another part of Las Vegas. Quickly, I proceeded to a Craps table that had gotten my attention. The stickman was repeatedly shouting, "Seven out!"

I watched the game for a while until the new shooter rolled a few numbers and sevened out. Immediately, I bought some chips and began to make bets on the Don't Pass and thereafter on the Don't

Come. Within an hour I was ahead around $8,000. The payoff man kept hinting that I should make him a bet as a tip.

"I'll have a much better idea how much to tip you when I'm through winning," I told him. "I wouldn't want it to be too little."

In a few minutes the shift boss came over to express his curiosity about me and the loss of his chips.

"Are you from Las Vegas?" he asked right in the middle of my winning streak.

"No, I'm from a city far away from here," I said.

"Well then, where are you from?" he asked.

"I hate to tell you," I said, "but actually I'm from Hoosierville! And I'll be staying until I'm through winning."

Soon, most of the other bettors quit playing. The two who stayed decided to switch and bet on the Don't side. Take my word for it, that was no table for Pass and Come bettors. I won for another half hour—and so did my two new friends who decided to bet the proper way—on the Don't Pass and Don't Come.

When the winning trend was over, and I lost a few bets, I left and walked over to a near-by Blackjack table, where luck was with me again. When I looked toward the Blackjack pit, I noticed the same shift boss pick up the phone. Before I was ahead a measly $500, company arrived. An obnoxious-looking woman, who was wearing imitation diamond jewelry that appeared to have come directly from the hotel's lost and found department. On her first hand, she stayed on Ace-4. That's a 5—and no one stays on 5. I could only suspect that she was a house shill and was sent to kill my streak. So, my only way out of this was to give her a $5 chip for her efforts. It was now definitely time for me to leave and get some sleep.

I stopped betting and ordered a drink from a cocktail waitress who was handling the area. When she brought my cognac I reached without looking and picked up a chip as her tip. I thanked her and threw the chip in her tray. I was surprised when I noticed it was a black chip ($100 value). The cocktail waitress thanked me with a quick nod. Then she noticed the chip's value and dashed away, looking up toward the ceiling, thanking her lucky stars. It was that night that I nicknamed her "doughnuts"—simply because she was nuts about my dough.

After I cashed in, the shift boss with two security guards followed me all the way to the door to make sure I departed their vulnerable establishment.

Before I went to bed I counted $38,000, which had begun with an original bet of $2.

The way certain casinos operated back then was in many instances a lot different from the way many new corporate establishments operate today. Also, the Gaming Commissioner and the Gaming Control Board's representatives enforce many rules limiting the various tactics applied by the specific sorcery masters of some establishments. In other words, the agitation, when I was most active, has lessened considerably. But regardless of this, some of the old traditional tactics did not change entirely in all casinos. As long as authorities are available to investigate matters, they will most likely have reports to evaluate at their desks. (My major purpose in explaining the few situations which I have experienced in the past is to inform and instruct the readers to be always alert when playing at a professional level.)

Gambling in big cities is where the potential for winning large sums of money is a major consideration for players who have reached a professional level. Most big cities are visited by businessmen who enjoy gambling in the evening hours, to relax and pass their time after a busy daily routine.

New York City was rated "number one" on my list during my gambling career. The hotels there bring in the most select clientele of businessman from many nations, and from all over the United States. The majority of these travelers have seen New York City and the sights during previous trips. If these entrepreneurs are staying at any of the hotels for a period of a week or longer, they become bored with nothing to do in the evening. Most commonly, they visit the hotel's bar at cocktail time. Later, they dine in the restaurants. Being a registered guest is a most natural way to make contact and engage in conversation with these men. Many of them enjoy meeting a young, bright businessman, and frequently games such as Poker, Blackjack, and even Craps are easy to arrange.

I had been in New York City for a few weeks enjoying a vacation away from Las Vegas. As usual, I visited several of my acquaintances and friends. One day at my hotel's bar I met two men who mentioned gambling in Las Vegas. They were interested in hearing that I was from the western part of the country, and that I had also visited Las Vegas many times. After much gambling conversation, in which all their winning trips to Las Vegas were mentioned, I learned that one of the men was a French clothing manufacturer, and his friend was a buyer. As the conversation continued I pulled out a wad of hundreds (about $20,000) from my pocket. When the two men spotted the sheaf of bills they glanced at each other and smiled. In only a few moments both men tried to persuade me to join them and some other friends for a private game. Amused with their fascinating idea, I agreed to give it a try. The manufacturer excused himself to go and contact the other players.

Nearly an hour passed before the manufacturer and his select group of four men arrived to join us. After the introductions were made, the manufacturer excused himself to purchase a few decks of cards from the gift shop. Soon, he was back and joining in the conversation. He explained that there were several games with which we could entertain ourselves, and offered us the use of his room. The majority of the men opted for Poker. After a brief discussion of the house rules we rode the elevator to a large suite.

All of the men were armed with small caliber bankrolls of cash, traveler's checks, and even cashier's checks. For the first few hands I remained quiet and observant, folding most of my undesirable hands, until I had a fair notion of how each of the men played. It wasn't long before everyone loosened up and the stakes rose. During this period I managed to win almost $2,000. Then, when most of the men were involved in the pot, I played out a poor hand purposely, losing most of the two grand. From that point on I always had a caller when I bet a winning hand.

At one point the manufacturer commented that he was beginning to feel hungry and thirsty. He suggested that he should call room service for a few sandwiches and a bottle and some mix. To that offer I agreed, very aware of the fact that with drinking even a winning player's good luck can become remarkably short.

Miraculously, after a few hours of play the modest gambler Pete the Greek had more than $10,000 in winnings in front of him. After suffering steady losses, the four guests decided to call it a night.

"Maybe tomorrow night we can meet again for another game!" one of the men said as they walked out of the hotel suite.

The clothing manufacturer and his friend the buyer, however, had not been convinced of their luck so far and insisted on continuing. I suggested that we change the game to Blackjack, since only three of us were left. (Two players against one can improve their chances by using cooperative skills at Poker.) They were both anxious for additional gambling adventure, so they were not hard to convince. To my surprise, they were concerned as to who was going to take over the Bank and cover the action. They were eager to play. Since most of the cash was stacked in front of me, I offered to cover their action.

The buyer appeared to know more than the basic rules of the game, but the Frenchman was totally innocent of the techniques of Blackjack. The two friends even got into verbal disputes several times as to why the other played so foolishly. Meanwhile, they were betting no less than $100 per hand, continuing to contribute their funds to me with remarkable determination.

In less than two hours they were both out of cash—but willing to write checks, which I felt would clear their bank. My response to their offer was that the game was to be a friendly one—and that they had experienced enough bad luck for one night. Perhaps meeting the next evening with some new decks of cards would be a better solution. Both men thanked me for being considerate, and accepted a $500 loan I offered to each of them. Their new concern was for tomorrow, as they made me promise to meet them at the bar early the next evening. Under the circumstances, I gave them my promise that I would be there. Going directly to my room I counted over $27,000 in profit. It was almost four o'clock in the morning when I retired, thinking that my winnings were the result of little effort indeed if compared to my Las Vegas activities. I felt very pleased by the fact that I was accepting the Blackjack action in the role of the casino without the overhead.

The next day, after a relaxing lunch with a lady friend (a very dear New York acquaintance), I met my new gambling friends. As I approached their table I became aware that I was the topic of their conversation.

"Hello lucky, come and join us!" said the French manufacturer and politely waved me over.

"Have a seat…please!" the buyer greeted me.

"Gentlemen, how was your day?" I politely asked, "Business go well?"

"Personally, I made big progress," the Frenchman answered. "As usual, I profited greatly."

"Splendid news," I said.

"How was business for you today, Pete?" the Frenchman asked in a curious but polite manner. "Are you positive you do not wish to join us in the clothing business?"

"As you gentlemen can see from the clothing I choose to wear my taste is quite special," I answered. "You gentlemen should be pleased I chose a separate career from yours…because I could be quite competitive in that field. But we all have our own specialities."

"Perhaps you're right, Peter," the buyer said grinning. "With your luck maybe it's just as well you're not competing with us."

From this point on, none of them were interested in discussing business. Their only concern was how soon we would begin the game.

My experience in devising strategies gave me an edge over my opponents again, even though they fancied themselves experts. I became good friends with all the players and exchanged addresses with the buyer and the clothing manufacturer. As it turned out, the two never seemed to tire of my performance each evening, which progressed into much higher action games two months later at a hotel in Southern California.

Surely I felt a little regret for winning a fraction of my opponents' fortunes, but I knew that if they won so much as a C-note from me, we would never hear the end of how clever they had been to outwit me.

During my travels to the east coast, I would occasionally visit a friend whom I first met in Denver during the early 1970s. He was an Australian-born American and one of the nation's most famous political cartoonists. The talented Patrick Oliphant had recently relocated to the nation's capital during the mid-seventies. He had resigned from the *Denver Post* and accepted an offer from the *Washington Star*, as obviously enough, political cartoonist.

One evening while we were dining at a fine restaurant, Pat introduced me to the operator of the establishment, who joined us for an after dinner liqueur. It wasn't long before gambling became the topic of our conversation. The well-known restaurateur explained that he had lost fortunes at Craps and betting on sports events. After expressing my sympathy, I asked him a simple question, the answer to which categorizes most players.

"Sir," I said, "would you please tell me how many combinations a pair of dice is capable of?"

He was a little puzzled, and embarrassed, as he thought and finally shook his head and said, "Pete, to be truthful with you, I don't know."

"Why did you risk such huge amounts of money at Craps without first knowing the basic facts of a pair of dice?" I couldn't help asking, but in a polite voice. "Each die has six sides...so 6 times 6 equals 36 combinations.

The restaurant operator looked thoughtful. This was the first time he had given thought to a simple fact concerning the game. Oliphant, fascinated, remained silent. I then offered a short but precise analysis of Craps. Since the restaurateur seemed to appreciate my advice, I continued by giving him my own recipe for Shrimp Provençal, to add to his menu. Thus, Oliphant and I would visit the restaurant frequently on a favored basis, since Pat is a vegetarian and needs special attention.

Later, I explained to Pat how difficult it was for me to understand such a gambler as the restaurateur. His attitude toward gambling puzzled me. "Why would someone supposedly intelligent," I asked, "plunge so deeply into something he knows nothing about?"

The same question has remained a mystery to me about many gamblers I have watched throughout the years, in private and casino gambling.

One evening I was invited to dinner by a good friend and occasional gambling companion, an entrepreneur nicknamed Trucko. He had been recently involved in a short-lived engagement, and was celebrating his separation with a new lady friend. The other invited guests were a Texas oilman, a contractor, myself, and our female companions. During dinner, the contractor began to tell gambling stories, which were wilder than his previous construction stories and even some of his fishing stories. Still, though, we all listened with patience and laughed politely at the end of each anecdote he related.

Throughout this ordeal the contractor had to be corrected a time or two by—who else?—his closest listener, of course, me. At one point he spoke with authority about the science of probabilities, connecting that field with the law of averages. Therefore, I had to explain that the law of averages was not a scientific theory. Feeling his statement challenged, he continued to insist that in gambling there was definitely a law of averages. Also, that it played a giant role and had significance in connection with the games played in Las Vegas.

I added my own comments to this theory. I explained that his law of averages, would not in any way force a pair of dice, the cards, or any wagering tool to perform differently. Then I added that I always gambled using statistics and the theory of probability as an essential element in games of chance. The contractor continued to disagree with me. In return, I could only tell him that he was welcome to go to college and major in the law of averages. This comment left him in deep thought. Then I told him that he would have one hell of a time locating a professor in any college to teach him all about this "law of

averages." Personally, I would continue to use statistics and probability which is a part of science and technology. At the end, I
emphasized that the many colleges available would offer numerous
professors for that field.

Naturally, not taking kindly to my analysis, he insisted that he
would teach me a quick lesson. He wanted to test my nerve and
courage on the spot by flipping a coin with me for $100. Without
hesitating I accepted his challenge. I pulled a hundred dollar bill out
of my pocket and put it on the table. After matching my bet he
flipped the coin, which landed on my call of heads. Figuring I had
won the bet I reached to collect the two Benjies from the table. The
cunning contractor, though, had other ideas. He insisted on doubling
up his bet for one more flip of the coin, to prove that his law of
averages was indeed a correct theory. I agreed to flip one more time
and guessed heads again. The coin ended up heads for the second
time. The contractor insisted that we flip for a third time. Having
hardly any choice, I guessed heads again and won the third bet.
When I reached for the $400, plus my original Benjie, the contractor
wanted one more toss. I explained that I wasn't going to let him
double up indefinitely. He, however, demanded that I give him a
chance to prove his point, and threw an additional $800 on the table.
To his chagrin, I won the fourth bet! The contractor's face turned
pale, as he counted out what appeared to be his last $1,600 on top of
the existing pile of cash. One more time the coin turned up heads
and I won again. After examining both sides of the coin the
contractor was in a state of shock. He asked in a low voice to flip
once again on credit.

By this time, Trunko and the other guests were awestruck
watching the contest.

I warned the contractor that it would be best to stop this madness
and quit. I even offered to give him his money back because we were
good friends. He asked Trunko to lend him money, but the answer
was a polite "no."

Then, Trunko ordered a round of drinks, and suggested that we
quit. They all toasted my good luck and drinks were quickly

consumed. In fact, the contractor's drink disappeared in one gulp. Then he tried to cajole me into flipping one more time, explaining that his credit was good. I told him to go for it—and guessed heads again. The contractor couldn't believe it: he had lost for the sixth time!

From this point on, there was no stopping. The contractor desperately wanted to prove his law of averages theory to the crowd. By now, everyone in the dining room (including the restaurant's staff) was watching. I personally didn't care because I had only a hundred invested in the first place. The contractor, after losing the fourteenth coin toss in sequence was ready to bet his entire construction company.

That's when I told him I quit—and that there was no more betting. I explained that I had given him more action than any casino's house limit would allow. Still, the contractor wanted to flip again, to demonstrate nothing but his own obsession with the so called "law of averages."

Unexpectedly, my friend Trunko reached out, picked up the coin, and flipped it one more time. The coin hit the glass on the table and then rolled all the way to the floor. This was the first time it turned up tails.

"You guys are even," Trunko said with a laugh. "We are the best of friends...and shouldn't be gambling against each other!"

I responded to his suggestion, because Trunko is a friend of long standing. He is the kind of friend who is extremely rare by today's standards. From the beginning to the end of someone's gambling career, real friends like Trunko are rare indeed. You can count them on one hand, and you may find, that you have a couple of fingers left over. As for the contractor, he's forgiven.

When money is at stake the true personality, character, attitude, and vulnerabilities of a person comes out more clearly than at any other time. A loser keeps on betting, no matter what happens, without showing concern or enforcing the various rules. The professional gambler would lessen the size of his bets or withdraw from any game when he was losing. Most commonly, and always opposite to the loser's behavior, he will show no hesitation in betting his money when winning. Then he would bet till he was sure that the winning period had completed its cycle. A frequent winner has acquired his knowledge the hard way, and is aware of the only purpose in approaching any game. His intention is not just to play—but to win. This individual has money management plans, which are the key to the heavenly gates.

The first few bets should be considered a test to sample luck, a short test to investigate the direction in which the cards or dice were falling. It's worth mentioning that if he was to win from the start, the experienced player would attempt to load his rack with as many chips as possible during his winning period. On the other hand, if this player were to lose the first few bets, he would quit and walk away from the table. This particular strategy is commonly known to professional gamblers as "hit and run." To practice money management is a tough task that even professionals often fail to perform properly. By failing to accurately gauge the above system a bettor has nothing to look forward to other than the self-punishment of defeat.

I rarely pay compliments, but many years ago I met a boxer who was the best fighter I have ever seen to consistently enforce a hit and run method against his opponents. Who else could he have been but the former heavyweight and three time champion of the world, Muhammad Ali (then known as Cassius Clay). The swiftness with which he handled an opponent was no mystery to me, ever since his first fight with Denver's own former world champ, Sonny Liston. This is why I backed Ali with all the money I could get my hands on before their second fight. (Liston fought Clay in an attempt to regain the world championship.)

It was during a lunch with Sonny Liston that I first met Joe Louis. (Since then I had seen both former champs on a regular basis because they practically lived in Las Vegas. Sonny stayed at the Flamingo, before the hotel operated as the Flamingo Hilton. Joe Louis stayed at Caesars Palace, where a statue was built in his honor.) Sonny invited me to his table to meet Joe. The two were having a heavy discussion, since a third heavyweight was the topic of their conversation. Sonny's concern was Cassius Clay, the dynamic new fighter who had come into the boxing world young and fresh from the Olympics. When I joined them the two big men were sitting in a booth. At first I expressed to Sonny my sympathy about his recent loss to Clay. Sonny acknowledged this with one of his own looks and a hint of a grin beneath his thin, dark mustache. To humor both giants I explained that I had heard of many people catching a fly with their hand before, but never had I heard of anyone killing a fly with his fist. Sonny and Joe both grinned. They were aware that I was speaking about Clay's speed and his general approach in the ring. Joe Louis assured me that Sonny was commenting on the same subject just prior to my arrival. Sonny's eyes were focused directly on Joe and he was occasionally glancing my way, as he continued to explain that in the ring Clay was constantly on the run. He was too fast for any fighter to keep up with. Then he went on with how Clay kept his distance, and when he closed in, he was also flying. If only Clay would stand still for a second, he was sure he could hurt him, Liston commented.

Sonny never smiled much, and when he finished talking, there was an undercurrent of irritation barely showing as he shook his head. That in itself was enough for my young eyes and brain to calculate the odds on the next fight, scheduled between Liston and Clay. Clay, of course, won the fight with an early knockout.

Hopefully, I have convinced you to follow the hit and run method. It not only pays off, but it will keep you out of trouble. In addition, it will allow you to put the money you could have lost to good use at a later time, when you come to a winning table, where you may discover that it's your turn to *hit* and not *run*.

When gambling, an economic crisis is usually the result of a player's self-deception and his lack of perception of various deviations from this norm. In order for a player to become a winner, all he needs to do is study and practice.

Chapter 6

Casinos and America's Future

During peak hours a casino can become bedlam. The clanging and banging noise from the slot machines is constant and the cacophony from the tables can attack a serious player's nervous system. And with music in most places, a player is hard put to keep his emotional cool. A very busy casino has never suited my style of playing.

Casinos are purposely designed to keep crowds wandering through them. Few "drop in" customers have a real reason for being at a specific area. Among them, there is a group of observers who like to make comments about other players' wagers. In fact, the number of know-it-all professors who walk from table to table explaining to their spouse or other bystanders how most betting is handled and why is pretty high. They rarely know what they are talking about, particularly when they attempt to explain the reasoning behind various bets and the system in working the Don't Pass and Don't Come angle in Craps. The number of times I've heard that I was betting *against myself* could fill pages. After they are finished with their explanations, it never fails (nine times out of ten), they walk to a nearby slot machine and proceed to lose their dollars.

The bulk of most casino space is reserved for that certain profit-producing device: the slots. There are many types of machines with various flashing lights and noisy music. Luckily the noises, which vary from loud ringing to musical or even siren sounds, only blast off when the machine pays off. However, I would hate to hear a reverse version and have to listen to each machine laugh, or whatever, every time it keeps the slot player's money with no pay-off. Several of these cleverly designed "one-arm bandits" even wish the slot player "good luck" before he or she inserts a coin. Casinos thrive on them. Some slot players are also very possessive of their own machines. Heaven protect anyone who tries to play or accidently touches their favorite one. Since the slots were invented, knowledgeable gamblers don't go near them, and warn others to stay clear of such hopeless wasting of money, but few players listen. Slot players will be the first to say that the machines cannot be beat consistently because they are built to bring in profit. But don't ask them why they are playing one while explaining these facts to you. They will also tell you that machines are the biggest sucker action next to Keno (which we'll get into shortly). But at the same time, they continue to push coins in the machine, with fingers blackened from the silver.

"It's rather an expensive way to build up your muscles!" a lady once taunted her husband. "How can a man your age sit there and watch all that fruit spinning? I have no idea! Why don't you save our money and take me to a show?"

I was walking by when I heard that particular statement. After a few moments of consideration, I walked back and offered them tickets to see the performance. Since I was comped, I signed the tab for the couple. In the showroom, I told the gentleman that the only way I could see him coming out ahead when approaching one of the slots would be if he attacked the darn thing with a bucket full of tools, rather than the bucket full of silver he was holding. After a laugh I politely excused myself and left the showroom.

The next major section in the casino is reserved for Blackjack. The average unskilled player has about a 10 percent disadvantage at this game of many techniques. Next in popularity is the dice pit. Poker seems to also hold a sizable area in many casinos, for the rake deducted from each pot brings big profits from the numerous tables.

Another section is reserved for Keno. At this game the chances to win are pretty slim. They say Keno was invented in China and I wish the idea was kept there and had never caught on in this country. I do know of a Greek word pronounced keno, however, which means empty space. We are all aware of something that never happens out there in dark and endless space, and that's winning at Keno. The odds of winning $50,000 are heavily weighted against the player. In other words, there are fortunes bet for each $50,000 rarely paid out. You would never throw a dollar away in the trash can, so why should you bet it on Keno to experience a similar feeling. Please don't laugh, because it's always sad to see that as we are entering the twenty-first century there are still so many people who take this game seriously.

During the last decade Sportsbook areas are being installed or enlarged because of the current sports-mania in this country.

Last in most casinos' space allowance comes Baccarat and Roulette, which is smaller only because those tables are not as well attended.

At the various tables you have the dealers, then the pit bosses who watch the dealers, the players, and boxmen who watch all transactions. There are also shift bosses who keep an eye on the scene. Let's not forget the cameras or mirrors over each table. After each dealer's shift, he or she will automatically clap their hands to show that no chips went with them. The number one rule in this industry is the honesty by all employees. They are trusted—but also carefully watched.

Some players, after a run of losses, may resemble living robots. After going from one machine to another and from table to table they manage to leave Las Vegas penniless. If their behavior is mysterious, the answer is not: they know nothing about gambling. My advice to such a player has always been the same. He or she should ask someone who understands the games to teach them the fundamentals. Another logical step toward winning, or for a gambler to acquire the knowledge to hold his own at the tables, is to purchase a good guide to gambling before he steps foot inside a casino. The few dollars he invests on the book in most cases will curtail losses and perhaps allow him to do some collecting.

A different type of gambler, ironically enough, is always looking for bargains, such as finding a casino with a $2.00 steak breakfast or a

$4.95 buffet. But he never stops to realize that the breakfast actually cost him $100 on slots and the price of lunch was several hundred dollars at Blackjack or Craps. However, if this player had a good idea of how the games are played and how casino establishments operate, he would stand a much better chance of winning, and regardless whether he won or lost, he could always ask for a comp ticket to cover meals for himself and a guest at one of the restaurants in that hotel.

A different type of gambler is someone who walks to the various Craps tables looking for a high roller with a few thousand dollars in chips in front of him. After watching the bettor accumulate some winnings, this individual believes the high roller has some secret skill in beating the odds. Then, after forming additional mental images about himself, the spectator buys some chips and begins betting the same way. By doing this, he believes he will impress the high roller and the other players who by now are watching him speculatively. The sad part of this idea is that it can cost a lot of money for any player who wants to maintain a high profile. The other unfortunate story behind all this, however, is that casino bosses value a comped guest according to his playing time (money turnover) at the tables, and particularly, by the size of his losses.

The winning methods and the money management rules mentioned previously are the only successful ways for a player to come out ahead consistently.

From early on, licensed casinos in Las Vegas have been built on profit, despite the long distances between this area and many large areas on the east cost. Nevada politicians recognized this. It is my opinion that for that purpose they initially decided to permit casino licensing only in the desert of Nevada. In my estimation, not a single vote by a politician was cast during those years with the intention of seeing the current expansion of gambling. The original purpose for allowing gambling only in the state of Nevada was to permit licensed casinos to operate in an area far away from heavily populated cities. This supposedly prevented the country's everyday working person from visiting Nevada on a regular basis, but at the same time brought money from all other states to Nevada to facilitate the growth of that state. If these were their original intentions, perhaps to some degree they were correct. Because the boom that followed has sparked the growth of Nevada's cities. It also contributed toward the completion of various freeways and further development of Hoover Dam, which prior to 1935 was known as Boulder Dam. Many years later legalized casino gambling was permitted near the most heavily populated area of the United States, in Atlantic City. It will be interesting to see how this affects the weekly pay check of specific individuals who previously visited Nevada perhaps once a year.

Another temptation affecting the average workman's paycheck is the increasing number of state lotteries. It's amazing that a certain group of people will wager their money on almost any proposition that is offered. Surprisingly, state lottery existed only in one state, New Hampshire, only as far back as 1964.

An additional attraction to the public and an encouragement to the needless expenditure of the hard-earned dollar is the licensing of additional gaming areas. States like Montana, South Dakota, Colorado and twenty-three others have voted to permit casino-type gaming.

The result of all this legalized gambling is undoubtedly costing the public more billions annually than the entire sum originally spent in Nevada casinos. My guess is that if gambling continues to grow at its present speed, its proceeds could exceed $450 billion annually by the end of the century.

As a final observation, less than half this enormous figure will be invested in state lotteries across the U.S. Legal and illegal bookmaking, card rooms, horse and dog track mutuals also account for a portion. Even a long-forgotten game like Bingo, which is meant mostly for older ladies to pass their time, will involve a staggering figure surpassing $5 billion.

All the above-mentioned, of course, is only a starter or an appetizer to the $450 billion gourmet dinner. The main course of this humongous banquet will be consumed by the group this book is talking about: The Legal Casino Gambling Empire.

Chapter 7

Gambling Probabilities and Characteristics

You must use your gambling stake for small action, while observing the direction in which your cards or dice are falling. Remember, you can lose several small battles sampling your luck, as long as your goal is to win the war in the end. Gambling consists of winning strategies and an assortment of money management skills. You must also possess the discipline of a winner, which means the ability to stop when you are losing and walk away from the table. You will discover that half the battle has been won if only you can avoid gambling after experiencing a losing streak. However, when you begin to win, you should bet high at the same table until the streak is over.

When you're losing, be afraid of the Monster! But when you're winning, always make sure that the Monster is afraid of you!

If you're going to gamble, you must first recognize the difference between a winning and a losing trend. When you lose two or three bets in a row, win one, then lose two or three more in a row, whatever the game may be, it's clearly telling you in its own language that you're losing. You've got to walk away from the game immediately and not wager a single chip till you feel lucky again. Then, as you sample your luck from time to time, it could take a day, a week, or even longer before you may begin to win again. You must recognize this at once or else you'll be contributing your bankroll toward adding more wings to the hotel's layout.

A professional loser is a person who goes from table to table and from one casino to another, without any plan and making excuses for his losses, while utterly exhausting his diminishing bankroll. He blames everything but himself—the world is against him. Anyone would agree he is absolutely correct in that assumption—so far, that is. What he fails to realize, though, is that there is a stubborn trend acting against him, and it's definitely time to take that long break and stop betting. No gambler can win with a confused and clouded mind, and especially without the help of winning sequences. This type of player is probably the one who believes in the law of averages. Unfortunately for the poor soul, there is no law of averages in gambling. Only God knows how many millions have been lost by poor souls who have backed, with their chips, this senseless myth. Their law of averages can only mean that all wins and losses must follow specific or definite short series and patterns without any sequences. If that assumption were true, then it would mean that if a person were to flip a coin 100 times, it would land once head and then tails as long as he chose to toss the coin. Any child would surely win at a game like that, every single time. The odds on how cards or dice fall are defined only after a succession of events—but there is no law that can specify a particular win or loss unless, of course, someone controls the event by cheating. Prior to a random toss of the dice, the particular event works on probabilities. Also, before a single card is dealt there is nothing that will indicate the particular value of the next card. The term law of averages—when applied to gambling—was first used in the prohibition era. The professionals were well aware that none of the amateurs who bet the various games they booked had any significant chance of winning. Therefore, the only explanation they instructed their bookies to pass on to their clients (the unhappy losers) was that sooner or later the *law of averages* would help them win and recover previous losses.

What really exists in all games of chance is the primacy of statistics and probability. To learn this one should be a student of mathematics or else read some of the many good books that offer enlightenment. Neither cards nor dice have any memory of what they did on the previous toss, yesterday or the day before, or any idea of what is to occur in the immediate future. Quite often, it takes several hours, days, even weeks for them to make a turnaround and begin to fall to your advantage. It takes patience combined with skillful strategies to take full advantage of winning sequences. By the time they occur, if you're gambling in a casino (where the edge is always on its side), your bankroll has probably been worked over to a point where there is little left of it. What I'm trying to make clear is that if winning trends are far apart, as at times they are, you must drop your betting action to the house minimum. If you don't, no matter how much money you have backing you up, it would not last long enough for losing trends to complete their cycle, especially if you are betting at a steady pace. The reason is obvious—the house edge, rake, juice, or whatever you wish to call it, is always working against you, slowly but surely. The choice is always yours and never changes. The casinos never force anyone to bet. They only offer a tempting environment in which to bet to suit the public's fancy.

So far, we have established why so much money is lost annually in casinos. The weekend gambler cannot become a steady winner, simply because winning takes patience and long stretches of action. The comp is another contribution to losses because it influences the player to continue to bet when he's losing. Successful gambling is rarely a weekend affair.

Even known high rollers have never consistently succeeded against the casino edge. Gambling constantly for a decade at Craps, even by betting where the odds are as close to $50/50$ as possible—which would be the Pass-Come or Don't Pass-Don't Come—is a losing proposition. Assume during that decade you witnessed 300,000 double sixes. That's only 100 of them per day, betting 300 days a year for 10 years. Even at $5 per bet, that's $1,500,000. At $100 a bet, it would be $30,000,000. As you can see, that kind of money is hard to make up in winning trends. There's no way possible to reverse the Law of Probabilities. You can't turn a minus expectancy into a plus one no matter who you are. The only future that awaits you is financial catastrophe. All this, though, is for only ten years.

What are the expected losses during someone's lifetime? The answer remains the same. In the long run, you will always find yourself on the wrong end. The more money you bet and the longer you play, the more you can expect to lose over the long haul.

The more you keep winning the more you should keep sampling or betting. On the other hand, the more you keep losing or declining the less and farther apart you should be sampling or betting. Sampling is wagering a small amount of chips to allow you to find out whether you are climbing or declining. For instance, if you are winning repeatedly at different tables at an individual or a number of casinos, you're on a winning streak. You must keep on sampling as often as possible *with larger bets*. On the other hand, if you are losing or declining, you must drop the size of your bets and place your samples farther and farther apart. In other words, never allow yourself to get in the hole for a large sum of money at any single table. Understandably, the larger the loss, the harder it will be to recover. Never make the irretrievable personal mistake, to which every player is vulnerable, and can rarely control—that is, to chase previous losses with more money.

Since the odds are always stacked against the player, the sampling method should be used at all gaming sessions. The sampling method is used by chemists and other scientists to measure substances for which accuracy cannot be determined by weight alone. The sampling method is commonly used to measure the number of units contained in a single drop of water or other liquids.

Without making things sound difficult, sampling is like the polling for the Nielsen Report, taking a few numbers out of the population to represent the whole.

Gambling when the odds are at nearly even as in a casino game like Craps or even Blackjack, each bet should be considered similar to a coin toss. Let's assume you are attempting to discover the consistency of a coin. This means whether the coin's weight is exact or equal on both sides—in order, of course, to determine its equity. (At this point, I must emphasize that there is nothing equal, the same, or exact in our world. Not any of two coins, two rings, two

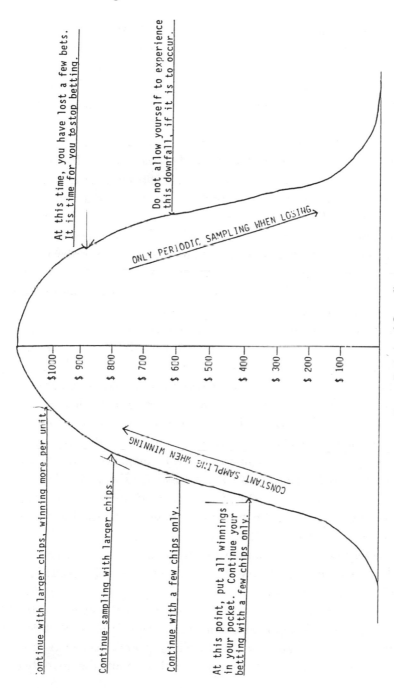

At this time, you have lost a few bets. It is time for you to stop betting.

Do not allow yourself to experience this downfall, if it is to occur.

ONLY PERIODIC SAMPLING WHEN LOSING

CONSTANT SAMPLING WHEN WINNING

Continue with larger chips, winning more per unit.

Continue sampling with larger chips.

Continue with a few chips only.

At this point, put all winnings in your pocket. Continue your betting with a few chips only.

$1000
$ 900
$ 800
$ 700
$ 600
$ 500
$ 400
$ 300
$ 200
$ 100

Fig. 1. Periods of Sampling

71

shirts, two purses, two atoms, even two nuclei and the number of protons within them. They may appear the same, but they are different units with their own identity.) The total sum of several hundred tosses of a coin should, in most cases, be sufficient to prove my point. A test of 100 tosses is considered a set. After reviewing the results of flipping the same coin 100 times for 10 separate sets and, the tails side prevails over the heads side on each set, you should have reason to believe that the heads side is the heaviest. In order for this experiment to make sense, you must first believe in the sampling theory, or else you'll be stuck with having to flip that same coin indefinitely only to achieve a similar result.

To also understand the meaning of trends, sequences, etc., you must recognize that nothing is guaranteed as to the order of the tosses within each set of your test. Take my word for it. The sequences within each set of 100 tosses will be different each and every time. The perplexity of this problem is, by far, greater than is commonly suspected. The problem is similar to a person attempting to figure out the winning numbers on a Keno board or in the state lottery.

The theory of probabilities appears to have been originated by Galileo Galilei. However, if we were to research further back in history, we would find out there were many other mathematicians who had also experimented with this theory. Even that far back in history, people were not ignorant as to the existence of the laws of probability. If human minds so many centuries ago were burning with curiosity enough to figure out this theory, why not today? Especially since we don't consider our present to be the Dark Ages. Why, then, are there multitudes of us so utterly unaware of it?

For the one who is planning to gamble and risk sums of money and valuable time, the theory of statistics and probabilities should be studied and understood.

Large companies in this country and all over the world, such as manufacturers of automobiles, televisions, tires, light bulbs, bricks, bolts, and screws all base their selling prices on the costs of production. How else could they accurately compute the quantity of materials to order, employees to hire, etc., including the size of the building of each manufacturer. Prior to figuring out their cost of the final product, all other facts must first be calculated. This plays the biggest role in setting the final price and presenting it to the consumer. Insurance companies also use the law of statistics and probabilities to determine all their costs and, thereafter, the premiums offered to their clients. Beforehand, though, they have taken the time to examine the statistics of fires, illnesses, deaths, and all policies written in the past. Therefore, by first examining the statistics, which are factual, they have a clear picture of future odds. What is to occur in the future may be evaluated by considering the statistics of past history. This is why you will rarely find insurance companies going broke, especially the large ones. The obvious reason is that these companies make it their business to first take into consideration all the foregoing. Most of you know of a phrase which has been used for their own safeguard and self-insurance. It's called "Act of God"! This phrase protects them from catastrophes and disasters that even insurance companies—with all their money backing them—could not survive if they ever had to pay off.

Returning to gambling (not that we ever left the subject) everything noted is one sort of wager or another and casinos have taken precautions similar to those of the insurance companies. One is the *house limit* and you find it in every casino. This protects them from having a very rich man walk up to a table and, on a single roll, breaking the joint. Another is the *house edge,* or percentage, which means that each game is structured never to pay off at true odds.

Take four pairs of dice, pick them up, shake them, and toss them so they roll for a short distance. I guarantee you that if you were to add the combinations of each pair, you will come up with the number 7 more frequently than any other number. There is a bit more to this, though. If you were to keep on tossing those eight dice many times over you will also discover at one point that, no matter how you add up the dots, the combination 7 will not appear at all. This should clarify what I mean when I mention the words trend, streak, sequence, etc.

Suppose that you are a manufacturer of a tire company and, furthermore, that you produce a million tires a week. As the one million tires roll off assembly lines there will be imperfections. Let's further suppose that you discover (and we'll stick to round figures) 2,000 material, machine, and manmade errors occur while these tires are being produced. However, there is no guarantee in what sequence the flaws will appear. It could be thirty bad tires in a row, then one good one, with ten bad ones to follow. Thereafter, you could have 50,000 good ones, with absolutely no flaws. You must understand that you are looking forward to approximately 2,000 malfunctions within the production of one million tires, but not the order in which these defects will appear. The only fact I will guarantee you, and I'm willing to bet all my money to your one dollar, the sequences of your damaged tires will be different every time for each million tires produced. The only chance you would have to win this bet is if you had *an infinite amount of time to produce tires*. Let me tell you what I mean when I use the word *infinite*: In order for someone to collect, he or she would have to live to do it in another world.

So please, don't take me or anyone else up on a proposition such as this one—because there simply is not enough money manufactured on this earth to grant you the payoff you deserve. You would have to multiply 2 times 2 equals 2 times 2—all the way up to a million. However, once this is accomplished, you still won't have the answer to all the sequences of all defects within the million tires. I guarantee you that you would run out of paper and pencil, if not out of figures, and especially patience. Even if you were to guess this impossibility once, you would still have no guarantee that the same sequence will ever come up again.

So, if the dice and cards are falling against you for a long period of time, all it means is that they are commencing a new trend or beginning a new direction separate from all previous events. They simply keep falling on your side or against you because they have no specific plan of their own. Therefore, the only chance you have to find out the direction they are falling is by using the sampling method for a short period which will allow you to detect the progress of sequences. Sampling periodically, with small wagers, will permit you to withstand bad times until you start winning. Then, and only then, if the wins are big enough and occur in a sequence as you move from one table to another, should you "go for the sky" by wagering larger bets. When you "go for the sky," make sure you always do it only with the house's chips you have already won; your own money is to be used for sampling your luck until you finally start winning.

A consistent loser never thinks of the foregoing. And, even when he reads everything and understands it all to some degree, he will not take the time to make any special effort to minimize his losses.

The problem with some players is that they were taught much faulty information about the fundamentals of most games. I don't want to give the impression that I'm perfect. I have deviated from the rules, and have paid dearly for my mistakes. If it seems I have repeated myself, it's only because I want to make sure you understand the difference between being a winner and a loser.

You don't get out of your bed in the morning, open the door, and empty your shotgun into the air just in case the ducks are flying by. You must first wait until you see the ducks. Then you shoot quickly and accurately, before they get out of range.

That's what gambling is all about. Or let me try this one on you: When you go fishing, you take the bait with you to catch the shark, you don't bring the shark along to catch the bait. This means you sacrifice a minimum amount of chips and bet low until something good happens.

If you can't abide by all these rules, do yourself the greatest favor in the world: Don't gamble.

Chapter 8

Craps or Hazard

Craps is the most fascinating game and the fastest action you'll find in a casino. This is my favorite game and the time I have spent at Craps in many parts of the United States outweigh by far all my other gambling times combined. Most people lose more money at this game by illusion than on purpose. The illusion, without any doubt in my mind, is the house cut, or percentage, which at a constant pace can exhaust a player's stake so smoothly it appears to be an unfortunate mishap.

A Craps layout is purposely designed with large numbers, bright colors, and high payoffs. This layout magnetizes the attention of those who are innocent of the true odds. The particular player who is attracted by such bright, colorful propositions (the Field, the Big 6, the Big 8, Hardway numbers, and One-Roll payoffs) is the exact prospect Craps layouts were designed to victimize. The Pass and the Come lines, accompanied by the Place Bet area, occupy the rest of the colorful Craps layout. However, the next time you're at a Craps table, compare the undersized areas provided for the Don't Pass and Don't Come bettor. These two areas appear microscopic, when compared to the other wagering choices. The purpose behind this placement was to frighten and discourage the bettor from approaching these betting areas. The Don't Come seems to be an out-of-the-way bet which cannot even be reached by most players. There just isn't enough room to comfortably accommodate the action of a few players' bets. Isn't it ironic, though, that the Don't Pass and the Don't Come bets carry the lowest house edge on the table?

The following display of odds is the biggest sucker action available on the Craps table. All you need do is remember to avoid them and tell other players to do the same. These bets neatly belong in the oblivion pigeonhole category of Keno, slots, or other machine apparatuses that keep casino owners singing. If the public should ever wake up and suddenly stop such contributions, they might cause casino owners to jump in their sleep. I'm against these bets; I've never bet them myself and I hope I never will. If I ever accidently catch myself betting this way, I would need no further convincing that I was beginning to show signs of inexperience. These bets do offer a plus, however: They inflame the emotions of the autointoxicated beginner.

TYPE OF BET	CASINO EDGE
Any 7	16.667%
Any Craps	11%
Big 6 or Big 8	9%
Hard 4 or Hard 10	11%
Hard 6 or Hard 8	9%
The Field	11%
The Field when aces or 12 pay double	5.55%
The Field when aces or 12 pay triple	2.75%
The two aces (snake-eyes) or 12 (box-cars)	14%
One roll 3 or 11	11%

Don't Pass

The contents of the following pages may be a little difficult for some to understand, but I am not trying to teach the beginner. My intentions are to instruct only those who already patronize Craps tables and will continue to do so.

The house advantage on the Don't Pass line is at its lowest, 1.402 percent. When a bettor lays double odds, the casino edge can drop to a slim 0.6 percent. With 10 times odds, the house advantage is the lowest found at any casino game today, dropping way down to triple zero figures, which is almost a non-existent house percentage. Regardless of what mathematics says, the original bet is still at 1.402 percent despite the fact that a gambler lays odds against a point. The odds laid are at $^{50}/_{50}$, but the original bet, prior to laying odds, is at

1.402 house percentage. The operators of casinos that accept 10 times odds count mostly on the errors of players and in the management of their bankrolls to gain profits. However, through busy Craps tables, these operators are also assured a jam-packed casino, as machines bring the operators tens of thousands in daily profit. I'm referring to only certain machines, not to all the glittering and rarely jingling slots available. In order to understand the following, you must be familiar with the game. As mentioned before, this book is not written with the intention of creating new gamblers or encouraging anyone to gamble.

If you've been betting the Pass Line and *placing* the numbers 4, 5, 6, 8, 9, and 10, you most likely have lost hefty bankrolls doing so. These bets never pay true odds. Unfortunately, there is no casino game that I know of that pays true odds. Surely, we are all aware of the fact that casino operators open their doors for profits. Therefore, they cannot afford to stay in business for long with the enormous investment they have in personnel, light bills, chandeliers, carpets, tables, free drinks, and dinners. Casino operators also have to meet the expenses of entertainment, advertising, executive management, and, of course, taxes. On top of all this, there is casino marketing and all the executives who work in those offices. These executives, and numerous other employees, book all conventions and cater to V.I.P. and M.V.P. clients. This means the hotels offer free trips or junkets (trips paid for by casinos, which includes air flights, complimentary room, food and beverage, etc.), tournaments, and all other promotions. In all fairness, these expenses mount to an annual total which varies from millions to tens of millions, depending on the scope of each hotel. You name the expense, they've got it, including the building that surrounds all this expensive package.

Throughout the years, my observations concerning hotel and casino profits have varied. The individuals with whom I have spoken have ranged from executives, casino managers, and a few owners. In addition to gambling, other profitable avenues have developed on the Strip. The profits in this area have moved from approximately 50 percent to more than 60 percent at casinos on the Strip. The highest expense is the cost of food (including the comp). The other burden on casinos' budgets is the high cost of free liquor, which fluctuated from 35 percent to as high as 60 percent, I've been told. (Since the addition of video Poker machines at bars, the liquor cost has gone much higher). The cost of salaries range from around 40 percent to 60 percent in some hotels on the Strip.

Unfortunately, for the casino industry, high overhead and all the aforementioned costs cannot be met at the low house edge of 0.6 percent (when laying double odds) from players betting the Don't Pass and the Don't Come. Therefore, those operators mostly depend on the everyday reliable casino cosmos, those who disregard the fundamentals concerning the house edge on Keno, machines, Blackjack, Baccarat, Poker, and Sports. For many years, casino operators have also depended on gamblers who are misinformed of the odds on bets at Craps.

Most people who play Craps bet the Pass Line and *place* the numbers. Casino payoff on placing the numbers are $9 to $5 on the 4 or 10, when they should pay $10 to your $5 true odds. On the 5 or 9 they pay $7 to your $5, when it should pay $3 to your $2 (which equals $7.50 for your $5 bet) in order to meet the true odds payoff. The 6 or 8 pays $7 to your $6, when the true payoff should be $6 to your $5. It appears that the house is keeping some profit on placed numbers. To some players, this constant deduction (house juice) seems relatively small. But after *placing* those six numbers for a period of one evening at $5 per bet, they've paid several hundred dollars in juice (hidden house advantage to the uninformed player), but still their luck ran even.

Almost always, losers blame their losses on bad luck. They fail to admit to themselves how fast those dollars add up. I would like to see the expression on the face of one such "intelligent" person (and by all means, a lot of them are, in their own fields) if the house had a cash register next to each table and rang those extra dollars up each and every time the dice rolled. That face would surely have a different look about it. Say a more thoughtful look? A thousand in the hole for one evening—and luck ran even! These are the types of gamblers casinos operators love to see line up at their tables. Undoubtedly, you know there are gamblers who bet against the odds, with bigger bets than the $5 bettor. Too many times, I've watched them, right next to me, lose thousands, while I felt sorry for them, and also helpless.

I've been playing in casinos for many years, betting thousands of dollars on each of my trips, but rarely have I ever seen the dealers smile. From the moment I make my first bet at a table, I notice the look in everyone's eyes. They don't favor the professional "Don't Pass–Don't Come" player. While you're betting on the Don't side and winning, your so-called "friends" (casino hosts) may be watching hawkeyed over your shoulders.

The only edge the house has over the "Don't Pass–Don't Come" player is the double-six (boxcars). In a private game, the double-six wins when betting on the Don't side. Thus, you are given an additional edge over the right bettors. Casinos bar the double-six for the Don't side bettor. This means they don't pay you but consider the comeout double six a "push." Some casinos in other parts of the U.S. bar double-aces instead (just to be different), which amounts to the same odds disadvantage.

The Don't Pass and Don't Come bettor can frequently during the game have the odds on his side. Just think, if the point is a 10, the Don't side has a 2 to 1 edge at that time. The Don't player can also enjoy a comfortable edge with any of the numbers he could have as a point, which are 4, 5, 6, 8, 9, or 10. The Pass and Come Line player *is always at a disadvantage*, and never has the edge at any point during the game. This is why I will not offer any particular way to bet on the Pass line, because there is nothing to teach on that side of the table.

By choosing to bet on the Don't Pass and Don't Come (using various betting structures), a player can actually turn the odds to his advantage. The logic for betting on the Don't side is that a player has various choices which a Pass and Come bettor does not have. These choices are explained in detail later in this book. Those are the several winning methods I managed to keep secret through the years.

First, though, I'd like to see everyone betting on the Don't Pass and Don't Come, aiming to roll a 7 as the dice are thrown after each point. The 7 can be made in six combinations, instead of the three ways to make a 4 or a 10, four ways to make a 5 or a 9, five ways to make a 6 or an 8. Betting on the Don't side forces the house to toss 4 or any of those other numbers twice before a 7 is rolled. I don't believe there would be any more games of Craps that could afford to be booked by today's casinos if everyone bet the Don't side and no other Craps proposition.

Then gambling would become similar to a horse race if the number 7 "Secretariat" was running against a donkey (a No Chance) number 4 and surprisingly lost to it. Most improbable. For many years, players have disliked my betting on the Don't side. They took my betting action as a personal grudge, that I was betting against them. After all, the house was booking my bet—so what did they have to worry about? The house paid each and every bet I won. As I've said many times, "I'd like to see every player switch and bet on Secretariat—then, automatically let the house bet on the donkey!"

I know it's no secret I bet on the Don't side, that the dice won't Pass. I know that if a shooter rolls a 7 or 11 on the comeout roll I lose. If he rolls two aces or ace-deuce, I win. (They bar 12, double-sixes, in Las Vegas.) But, if the shooter rolls a point—any of 4, 5, 6, 8, 9, 10—he'll have to match it again before he rolls a 7 or he loses. So let's understand that if a shooter rolls a 4 (a three-way number), he'll have to match it again before rolling a 7, or I win. Meanwhile, he has three combinations to match the 4 against the six ways a 7 can be made.

Suppose you bet $5 on the Don't Pass and the shooter rolls a 10 (which again is a three-way number) and you lay $10 odds against the 10. This is what you have so far: If you win the bet, you get paid $10 for your $15 total bet, while the shooter has only three ways to make the 10, but six ways to roll a 7 going against him. Admittedly, the shooter or Pass Line bettor had a small advantage to win on the comeout roll by rolling a 7 or 11 and your original $5 bet would be picked up. But the shooter had only one roll to accomplish this.

There are six ways to roll 7, two ways to roll an 11—that's eight combinations when the shooter is coming out. Against him, he has one combination for two aces and two for Craps (ace-deuce and deuce-ace) for a total of only three combinations. (Again, the Pass bettor loses when a 12 is thrown). The key here is (what most Pass bettors have not considered) that you, by betting on the Don't side, also have a remaining 28 combinations that the shooter can throw instead of a 7 or 11 on the first roll. There are a total of 36 combinations for a pair of dice, since dice have six sides. To explain further, the Pass bettor has 24 ways to come up with a point on the first roll, which are also working against him. The numbers a Pass bettor has to accomplish a point are any of 4, 5, 6, 8, 9, 10, which total to 24 combinations.

Explaining it yet another way, number 7 is on the Pass bettor's side for the first roll only. After a point is established, the 7 becomes your point (betting on the Don't side), until the shooter matches his point, or most likely sevens out. The Pass and Come bettor is always at a disadvantage after the comeout roll, no matter what his point is. Any of 4, 5, 6, 8, 9, or 10 two times, before a 7 rolls in between, is constant bad news.

The numbers a player can have as a point can be made in the following combinations. There are three ways to make a 4 or a 10, four ways to make a 5 or 9, and five ways to make a 6 or and 8.

Example 1:

Assume a shooter rolls a 5, which is a four-way number. That 5 is established as his point. In order for the Pass Line bettor to win, he'll have to match the 5 again before he rolls a 7 (a 6-way number). That leaves him with a 4-to-6 disadvantage, which makes a 3-to-2 advantage betting on the Don't Pass.

Example 2:

Suppose you have a bet on the Don't Pass and the shooter rolls a 7 or an 11, and your bet is picked up. The shooter had six ways for the 7 plus two ways for the 11 to win on the comeout roll. You, though, betting the Don't Pass, can win instantly with one combination, which is aces, and the ace-deuce that can be made with two combinations (ace-deuce and deuce-ace, because there are two dice). You also have three ways to make a 4; three ways to make a 10; four ways to make a 5; four ways to make a 9; five ways to make a 6; and five ways to make an 8. But he doesn't roll any of all those numbers mentioned (which add up to 24 combinations); he rolls a 7 and you lose. The shooter picks up the dice again, but this time, he rolls a 4. Suddenly, he has only three ways to make the 4 going for him (betting the Pass Line), but six ways to roll a 7 going against him. As a result, you know what happens now? The 4 seems to have gone on vacation. You couldn't find it with a search warrant.

Please don't misunderstand me, the 4 or any of the other numbers can be matched and often are, but never as frequently as they are not. If you happen to be at a table betting on the Don't, and the shooter throws two naturals (which are 7 or 11), you don't have to keep on betting against that same shooter—because what if he connects with 8 or 10 passes? Sometimes it happens. After your second loss, you simply wait until he's through shooting. There is always the next shooter to bet against.

So much for the Don't Pass for now. I believe you'll agree that it's the best side to bet your money on.

Don't Come

I'm just rolling the dice in front of me. First, I roll an 8, then I roll a 4, then I roll a 6, and then I roll a 7. Home run! What does all this mean? If I am betting the Don't Pass and thereafter the Don't Come, I get paid for the 8, the 4, and the 6, because those numbers were never repeated. There are twenty-four ways to roll 4, 5, 6, 8, 9, and 10. We also know there are six ways to roll a 7. If we divide 6 combinations into 24, what do we have? Mathematically, every time four of those numbers (4, 5, 6, 8, 9, 10) appear, a 7 expectancy is there. Those 24 combinations plus 6 ways for the 7 equal 30. The remaining combinations, which add up to the 36 a pair of dice consists of, you need not worry about. Betting on the Don't Come (similar to the Don't Pass) ace-deuce itself makes up for the 11, since they both are two-way numbers. The two aces remain in your favor. Casinos bar double-sixes (also on the Don't Come), which would be in your favor if they didn't.

Years ago, when Craps was played in alleys, basements, and attics, the sharper boys on the block ran games to bring in the chumps and hustle them by always betting against them. Simply because they knew that *betting wrong* without barring the double-sixes or double-ace has the advantage or edge. (The term "wrong bettor" was purposely invented by the fathers of prohibition, so players would assume they were doing something wrong by betting on the Don't side. "Right bettor" was invented only to lead chumps to believe they were betting the proper way.)

My next task is to explain the mystery of the dice game. Dice do not have a mind. But for a period of an hour, a week, a month, or let's just say the lifetime of a gambler, they sure as hell know what they're doing. The odds can actually work out to a fraction of a percentage—for you, or against you. It's only the long term, though, that will define the precise differences and determine the final outcome of the true percentages. The period of a game will at times deviate from normal progression, deceiving many players, particularly amateurs.

Going back to the Don't Come way to bet, pick up a pair of dice and try this yourself. After only a few tosses, you'll roll 7. Pass and Come Line bettors, after the comeout roll, hope to ditch the 7 on each and every roll, or how else can they survive? Most commonly, that doesn't happen—and that's how they end up going broke on damn near every trip to the tables. The essence of the Don't Come action is similar to the Don't Pass, but even better. The 7 again is the key and you have it working on your behalf every single time the dice are tossed after any of these numbers are thrown on the comeout—4, 5, 6, 8, 9, and 10. At certain times, you may have several bets on the backline, and the moment the 7 appears you'll win on all your bets. Throughout many years of gambling, while betting the Don't Come, I have doubled up on my bets (as some of the numbers were repeated). That particular way of betting should be executed gradually, thus exhausting the long rolls. There are times when a shooter may roll twenty or even more numbers before a 7 appears, but that doesn't mean you must bet against those rolls each and every time. If you lose a few bets, stop betting the Don't Come. Leave the bets that remain on the backline—and if they are all repeated, you can always bet against the next shooter, who may not roll as many numbers. (In most cases, I would double up on my bets. But only after a dozen or more numbers are tossed.)

If you wish to bring back your existing bets on the Don't Pass and Don't Come, it's up to you. In explanation, your Don't bets are not imprisoned by the casino rules, as they are on the Pass and Come Lines. Of course, by picking up your Don't bets, you'll be giving away the edge you already have. That's the only reason why casinos allow such a transaction in the first place.

Anyone who has gambled for as many years as I have undoubtedly has gambling experiences to recall and stories to tell. Once I was betting on the Don't Pass and Don't Come. While chasing the long roll, I was doubling up on the size of my Don't Come bets and losing heavily. The shooter on the opposite side of the table was a big man well into his thirtieth toss of the dice without a 7—and showing no apparent sign of ending my nightmare. This shooter had a single dollar on the Pass Line and, each time he rolled, bragged to a friend next to him about all the damage he was causing me. Meantime, I had several thousand riding on the backline, hoping for the 7 to finally appear and save me. Regardless of what the odds say, the dice had apparently forgotten that the 7 exists. Throughout this ordeal, my mind was indeed suffering but, as always, still functioning. I changed a chip to one dollar ones and threw one of them in front of the shooter hoping to distract his momentum. Eagerly, but still laughing, he picked up his tip, but in doing so he also lifted both dice to toss them across the table. The dollar chip, of course, stayed in his palm as the dice flew across the table.

"Touchdown...!" I thought, as the dice landed in front of me with a 6-1 on top.

A player doesn't have to always wait this long for a 7 to show, but at certain points of the game, the long roll can be expected. Another memorable occasion occurred when I had the company of Telly Savalas at a casino one evening. (My sister had recently interviewed the actor and had written a newspaper article on him a few weeks prior.) Telly chose to bet his usual way on the Pass and Come Lines. And, as always, I was busy placing Don't Pass and Don't Come bets. The previous understanding was that we both couldn't lose, since we were betting opposite each other. After all, the house was booking the action. Therefore, one of us was bound to win.

At one point (under a persistent long roll), Telly was beginning to win and I was building up my bets in the usual manner, and the backline was loaded with chips. The shooter was a woman (not too handy with the cubes) and as she tossed the dice one of them landed at a 6 rest point, but the other flew up, hitting another lady in the chest. This lady was wearing an extremely low-cut evening dress, and the die fell neatly into her cleavage. The surprised but smiling woman swung her upper body forward quickly. Her movement released the momentarily hidden die, which fell on the table with the ace side showing on top, and the 7 was called by the stickman. The ace *was the additional pimple* needed to clear the table.

Telly's eyebrows rose as he made an about face and walked away to play Blackjack. The humorous part of this story is that he was not performing an act. His lifted eyebrow was a short, painful reaction and it was for real, since all his chips quickly vanished.

Once, at a hotel in Atlantic City, I approached an unpatronized table which appeared inviting. My first bet was $5,000 on the Don't Pass. After picking up the dice, the first number I threw was a 4. I felt confident, since the 4 is only a three-way number. The second time I tossed the dice, though, I matched the little Joe (an expression for the 4) right back. This time I was the one who registered painful surprise with a risen left eyebrow. That particular table was to cost me a great deal more than that five grand.

Another unusual story is when I had a Don't Pass bet (this time only $500) against the number 5. At one point of the roll, one of the dice landed on the tablemat with a 4 on top. The other cube hit the wall and flew up high, landing on a single stack of chips in front of the payoff man, with the ace showing on top. The two combinations add up to 5 and my bet was picked up, leaving me dumbstruck.

This particular house rule is probably a once in a lifetime expectancy. When one of the two dice (or even both) land on the house's back chips, that roll is considered no action. That's the house rule in all Las Vegas casinos, and it happens quite often. However, the single stacks of chips, the *front chips*, which are in front of the payoff man, are considered live, and if (as in my situation) a die happens to land on that stack of chips, the play counts. The chips in front of the boxman are many stacks orderly bunched and all together. However, the single stacks in front of the payoff man stand separately on their own, and the odds on a die landing directly on that stack are pretty high.

A person who does not take or lay odds is not taking full advantage of the best house options. The professional gambler's cognizance of casino odds has advanced to a level where he understands that the evaluation of compounded decimals will always amount to a definite house edge with serious results to the bettor. Therefore, a precise knowledge of the odds, combined with money management rules, is the only means to successful results. For instance, laying 2 to 1 against a 10 is an intelligent way to bet, because the 10 is a 2 to 1 underdog, since there are three ways to roll a 10 and six combinations for the 7. Since the 7 is a 2 to 1 favorite, you lay $100 to collect $50. It's a 2 to 1 shot, and the odds will never change.

A simple way to understand the constant casino search for profit is to walk up to a table and ask a dealer to place a $100 bet on the *no* 10. In other words, that a 10 will not appear before a 7. They'll simply explain that it will cost an additional 5 percent. Casinos must have an edge on all betting, and when you take or lay odds, they are for free and should be considered an advantage. That's why this particular bet is called "free odds." The only way a casino will let you take or lay odds, though, is only if the wager is accompanied by a previous Pass-Come, or Don't-Pass–Don't-Come bet. You must have first placed a bet before laying or taking odds, so they can take their shot at you. This means they get a chance at your bet through the double-six on your original bet prior to taking or laying free odds. On the Pass and Come, if a 12 is rolled, your bet is picked up because it loses. On the Don't Pass and Don't Come, you get a *push* instead of getting paid. No matter which side you bet on, the house takes a 35-to-1 shot at all bets made. It may not seem like a heavily tilted edge, but add 50 of those twelves together in a period of a few hours. At $50 per bet, that's $2,500 the casino is into your bankroll, whether you realize it or not. We're right back at the house's hidden advantages over players who don't understand true odds.

The Don't Pass and Don't Come side of the table allows a player certain alternatives that the Pass and Come side does not permit. Once a point is established on the Pass or Come lines, any 4, 5, 6, 8, 9, or 10, the right bettor is always at a disadvantage. The Pass Line bettor has the 7 on his side for one roll only, which is the comeout roll. The rest of the time, after a point has been established the 7 becomes the Pass bettor's nightmare unless he matches his point.

Gambling is not for anyone who can't afford to lose. When gambling, you must have a sufficient bankroll to withstand dry spells of vanishing chips. If you had thousands deposited in your bank, and you decided to bet $5,000 of it, how could that possibly hurt you? On the other hand, if you had a few hundred or even three or four thousand dollars and took it all to a casino and lost it, of course it could be devastating. My advice is don't bring any larger amount of money to sample your luck with than you can comfortably afford to lose.

When a player walks up to a Craps table his first few bets should be winning ones. If he loses, he should reduce his action down to the minimum till he begins to win. A player who is willing to bet low when he's losing (even if he's wealthy) will never need anyone's sympathy regarding his losses, simply because he's an automatic winner, provided that he increases his bets when he's winning.

Craps or Hazard

A lot of money can be won at Craps, if one takes advantage of trends. Dice can run hot and cold several times during a period of a few hours. That's when money management is important. Money management plays the biggest roll in gambling and separates the winners from the losers. When betting at the same level, wagering the exact value on each roll, your chances of leaving the table with a profit are slim. The size of bets should fluctuate according to various wins and losses.

A perfect example is written in the Bible. "Plant a few seeds; if the seeds are good, they mature for a great harvest. However, if the seeds are not good, they will be eaten by birds or scattered among thorns, where the thorns will grow up to choke them so they will yield no grain." (Mark 4: 3-9.)

Repetitious? Perhaps! But, unfortunately, not repetitious enough for most gamblers who play Craps for high stakes.

I don't advise anyone to take up gambling. My advice, and the purpose for which this book was written, only instructs those who already gamble and will continue.

Always remember that the name of this game is not a *crap game*, as many entertainers have called it and sung lyrics about it for so many years. Also, never call a Craps table a *crap* table, as casino employees often do. The name of the game is Craps, which translates as "Hazard" in French, and that's the only name that properly suits this game.

Chapter 9

Blackjack

Casino customers are recognized by the staffs in the same way well-known patrons are known by the managers of hotels and restaurants. In return, casino employees are remembered by the customers. A dealer may be compared according to his conduct and overall efficiency, to the service of a good or poor waiter who has served you in the past.

It is difficult to categorize casino employees, as they constantly change and differ in their use and abuse of the house rules. I'll never forget one time, during a heated dispute with a dealer whose interpretation of house rules were exaggerated. To win his argument, this dealer signaled his pit boss over to verify his claim. The $25 bet I made for him earlier, which turned into $50, had been long forgotten, as in most tipping cases.

The pit boss, who was himself only a recent former dealer, was instantly concerned and walked over to investigate the dispute. He was wearing a red sports jacket enhanced by numerous big brass buttons, as if he were the general in command. Since I had known him for years, it appeared that the brass buttons of his red jacket (which he had worn damn near every day since his recent promotion) had become his medals of honor, and further evidence of his authority. He was puffing on a long, fat cigar (compliments of the house, of course). He certainly knew it all now.

The dispute was about my deciding to play two hands and insisting on looking at both hands before I made any decision to stand or take a hit. The dealer's argument was that I couldn't look at both hands. My own was that the second hand belonged to a girlfriend standing next to me and anxious to play. Therefore, either she or I (since I was her adviser) should have the right to look at her hand before making any decision.

Red Jacket's opinion was negative, since the bets were made *out of the same money*. So according to his personal rules, I had no right to look at both hands. My question to him was that since when was it a house rule that I couldn't give $1,000 to a young lady to play with? I had to go over Red Jacket's head and call for the casino manager, whom I knew, and who was in the vicinity. After a short but precise explanation, the casino manager (my old acquaintance) was convinced that I was in the right and I was permitted to look at both hands before making a decision to play. Red Jacket's face turned the same color as his coat. No sooner had the manager walked away than Red Jacket began to mumble words of warning. My reaction, as I stood up, was to call the manager right back.

"Hey, Confucius," I said with a grin (let's call him that for now, since he had the look of a sage), "Red Jacket over here has been acting pretty smart ever since he got promoted. I didn't know he had it in him. It must have cost the casino a fortune to make him this smart!"

"Yes, Pete, you're right!" Confucius answered with a smile. "He's moving up in class. Thanks to me, of course!"

Meanwhile, Red Jacket, assuming he was receiving a compliment, inhaled a breath of air so deeply, one would think his brass medals would surely pop off his jacket.

"Really," I continued, "since Red Jacket got promoted he's become quite a brain, hasn't he? Someone surely must have taught him everything...all the tricks in the book. Do you think if you were to search around town you could hire a specialist to teach him that it's not very wise to always pretend he's a walking Blackjack encyclopedia?"

Quickly, Red Jacket's posture slowly began to deflate—as everyone around the table, including Confucius, was laughing at him.

This story had to be told, for the reason that two players playing Blackjack together, and out of the same money, can enjoy an edge over the house. To remain unnoticed by the dealers, one of the players should walk into the game first and the other join a short time later. The playing period should be relatively short, of course. Also, the two bettors should never talk or even look at each other. In fact, they would be much better off to exchange a wisecrack or two as to why the other plays so foolishly. After these two friends are finished winning, they should always depart from the casino, walking out different doors. Personally, I've never attempted such strategy and I'm not suggesting or pressing this issue. I'm simply explaining that it can be done and the results are usually profitable. Throughout the years, I have witnessed this method repeatedly, and I'm positive it's being presently allowed in most casinos.

In mastering Blackjack, the aim of intelligent hitting is not to reach the count of 21, but to prosper from the dealer's automatic hitting. In other words, a player has options from which to choose which a dealer does not have. There are also techniques a player should be aware of in order to minimize the number of times he goes over. It is a house rule that the dealer must hit up to and including 16, and that he must stand on 17. This rule should be considered an advantage for the player. The biggest house advantage is that when you bust, the dealer collects your wager no matter what his hand is (even if he busts); he has already scraped up your bet. If the dealer had not collected your bet in advance, all ties, *including the busting part*, would have been a push. This is a house edge. Therefore, if the dealer has to take a hit, don't take a hit yourself when holding anything over 11. In order to keep this game as close to even odds as possible, you must follow certain rules.

Take a Hit

You take a hit when you're holding 12 through 16 and the dealer's up-card is any of 7, 8, 9, 10, picture, or Ace. When the dealer's up-card is any of 2, 3, 4, 5, or 6, he must take a hit, regardless of the count of his face-down card. Again, the idea is to improve a low-count hand till you reach at least 17—and that's only when the dealer's up-card is any of 7, 8, 9, 10, picture or Ace. Remember, every time you take an extra hit, it increases the chances of busting your existing hand—that is, reaching a count over 21. The expectancy of an average card, over a long period of hitting, will average out at 6.53.7. This figure, of course, is calculated with the Ace counting always as 1 and not as 11. In Blackjack, only one of the Aces dealt to you is allowed to have the flexible card count of either 1 or 11. A second or third Ace dealt counts as 1. Personally, depending on the situation, after having hit a particular low-count hand two or three times, if the card count is still 15 or 16 I would stand, fearing the next card may be any one of 7 through 10. In a situation like this, you may imagine that there are approximately 24 cards left which can make or help your hand, but there are 28 cards of greater value which will surely cause a bust. In summary, most of the time it's the fourth or fifth card that will bust you. This is why, initially, casinos had a rule (till several years ago) that a player got paid automatically when holding a total of five cards. The purpose behind this rule was to force a foolish player into taking unnecessary hits. This idea went out of style as card counting became more prevalent.

The worst cards a dealer can have facing up are the 4, 5, 6, and, in some cases, the 7. Undoubtedly, some will question the fact that the 7 is mentioned. For the dealer to have a pat hand of either 17 or soft 18, when showing a 7, is less frequent than one may believe. There are 16 ten-count cards, plus 4 Aces in a 52-card deck. This means there are only 20 ways a dealer will not have to take a hit, but 32 ways that he will. This amounts to a little over 3-to-2 disadvantage for the dealer to have a pat hand of 17, or soft 18, with his first two cards.

You should always hit a 12 (once only) when a dealer is showing a 2 or a 3. This is the only busting hand of your own that you should hit if the dealer *has to take a hit*, which is when his up-cards are any of 2 through 6.

Splitting

As a rule, casinos allow you to split pairs of equal value. For example, if you are dealt any pair of 2, 3, 4, 5, 6, 7, 8, 9, 10, through pictures or

Aces, you may split those cards and make a second bet alongside the original bet.

Only the self-destructive split pairs of 4, 5, 6, 9, 10, or pictures. The reasoning is quite simple, mathematically or otherwise. With two 4s, you can end up with an 18, which is better than the average hand. However, if you split the 4s, who knows what you'll end up with? Two 5s can result in a 20, or even 21, with a hit. Two 6s split could give you a result of two 16s, which are the worst hands you'll ever want to be betting your money on. A pair of 9s are already an 18, and who would want to chance otherwise by splitting them. And how could you split a 20? Well, there is one exception. That is, if you're a card counter and you're sure that the deck is loaded with 10s, pictures, or Aces—and only when the dealer is showing 5, 6, or 7. (The results are similar as when doubling down against the dealer's 5, 6, or 7.)

Always split Aces, no matter what the dealer shows. Unless, of course, you're counting cards and you're positive that the cards to be expected are *low count*. When splitting Aces, the odds are favorable for the player to win both hands with a 21 or less, or at least win one hand and, if you lose the other, get a draw or a push and break even. That's the worst you can expect the majority of the time, if you split Aces. An additional house rule on splitting Aces is that you only receive one card to each hand and no hits are allowed.

You split 7s only if the dealer shows 7 or under, because you may turn a 14 into two possibly good hands.

When splitting specific pairs, you're permitting yourself the flexibility of choice, because you're playing out two separate hands. Afterwards, the dealer may have to stand or take a hit, obviously with no choice at all.

Always split 8s if the dealer shows 8 or under.

You split 2s and 3s if the dealer shows 2 through 7, since you have a choice on what to hit and the dealer doesn't. Chance are, you will end up with two better hands than the dealer.

Always remember, the dealer's worst showing cards are the 4, 5, 6, and also the 7, which I mentioned earlier. When the dealer is at a disadvantage, this fact should always be considered during the play, depending on the situation.

Doubling Down

Here you will find that casinos allow you to double the amount of your existing bet. In return, though, as they always must have an edge, you only receive one card dealt *face down* to your existing hand. Even though the single card is dealt face down, you have the right to look at this card. It's always a good idea to see the value of that card, particularly when you're playing more than one hand. Doubling down requires very careful thinking, because the single card you will be dealt could leave you at a disadvantage. I would double only when holding a 10 or 11 (4 and a 6, 4 and a 7, 3 and an 8, etc.) and that would be only when dealer's *up card* is 8 or under. Never double down against the dealer's 9, 10 count card, or Ace, even if you're counting cards and the cards to be expected are 10s or pictures, because the dealer could also have a 10 under his 9 or 10 showing. Countless times I've witnessed players double down against a dealer's 10 count card or Ace showing and catch a deuce or three as a reward.

Soft Count

A soft count is an Ace accompanied by a 9 or lower. For instance, Ace and 2 equals 3 or 13; Ace and 3 equals 4 or 14, etc. I don't recommend that you stand on soft 17 or on any lower soft count, no matter what the dealer's up card is. The reason for this is that low soft counts can be improved with advantageous results over the dealer's hitting. By taking extra cards on a soft-count 12 through 17, you can expect a favorable outcome most of the time. The first hit, of course, will never bust your existing hand, but you can try to improve it. You should never hit a soft 18 through 20. The chances of improving those hands are very slim and only for the bettor who *thinks* he understands how to take full advantage of the odds.

My personal rule is to double down on a soft 12, 13, 14, or 17 when the dealer is showing 5 or 6. The soft 15 and 16 I play out accordingly. When doubling down holding a soft count, a quick calculation can reveal the answer you will need prior to making a decision. For instance, when holding a soft 12, any Ace, 2, 3, 4, 5, 6, 7, or 8 can help in turning your hand into a winner. These 8 numbers, times four suits, equal 32 cards which will not bust and can improve your existing hand. (The true count is actually 30, because you already have an Ace and 2 in your hand.) So the odds favor doubling down and could win twice the amount on this hand. The remaining 20 cards, 9, 10, J, Q, K, will not give you a great hand, but won't bust you either. Still, the dealer will have to take one or more hits with no choice at all, and most of the time (according to the odds) he will go over or bust his hand. This particular way to count is an important strategy to remember. The efficacy of this strategy can only be seen when the first hand is dealt and you're the only player at the table. The rest of the time, it becomes a hit-and-miss type statistic, but it's a good strategy to practice as you play.

Insurance

You should only buy insurance when you are holding Blackjack and the dealer's up card is an Ace. Even this rule should not be considered standard play when time to buy insurance arrives. One exception (which goes back to card counting) is if the deck is running rich with pictures or 10-counts. In this case, you should buy insurance and collect even money. However, if you believe that there is no 10-count card under the dealer's Ace, it would be to your advantage not to take insurance and collect on the 3-to-2 payoff that casinos pay on Blackjack. It makes better sense to do this than to get paid even money when you buy insurance. If I had a fortune riding on a bet I would take insurance, making sure I collected even money, regardless of my hope of collecting a 3-to-2 payoff. Never have I bought insurance otherwise, and I don't suggest that you do so.

Always remember that in order for the dealer to have Blackjack there are sixteen 10-count cards versus thirty-six others. This amounts to well over the 3-to-2 true payoff odds you should be collecting when having Blackjack. It also tells you that when showing an Ace the dealer won't have Blackjack by over 3 to 2. The odds become even higher when you consider the fact that you already have Blackjack.

Card Counting

I try to bet always at tables where single decks are used (now a rarity), because the chances of knowing what cards have been dealt or what cards are to be expected obviously become more apparent. My second choice would be a double deck, although the total time I have spent at such tables is minuscule. Unfortunately, most casinos deal out of a shoe. A shoe usually is made up of four or six decks. There have been a few casinos in Puerto Rico and elsewhere, far from continental U.S., which have used up to eight decks in a shoe.

Regardless where you play, casino staffs have been long aware of card counters ever since they originated in the early eighteenth century in the U.S. Today's management and their dealers are always on red alert for extremely good card counters or consistently winning players. They simply will not allow heavy wins or undesirable leaks by card hustlers. Most casinos use the six-deck shoe to prevent card counting. Therefore, if you're gambling at a table which consists of six decks, some of which are not in operation (the moment a dealer reaches his plastic marker he stops dealing), it is impossible to keep an accurate count. No player that I have known has been able to tell me what's in front or in back of the plastic marker. No matter what books on card counting you have read, management and most of their staff have also read them and have taken appropriate precautions. They always keep a close eye on the way you play. Also, the dealers watch the fluctuation of your bets. Even to a person with a photographic memory, successful card counting is a difficult process. If this person is a consistent winner, sooner or later (depending on management) he may be asked to leave and never come back.

The high/low method is another losing ploy when counting cards, and will not succeed either. The reason it won't work is because you can never be sure how large or how small the next card count will be. Also, who's to tell when an 8, 9, or a 10-count card will suddenly appear and bust your hand after a hit. Basing successful Blackjack betting on card counting and the high/low method combined is never enough. Card counting will, more frequently than not, complicate matters when having to make accurate decisions at the fast pace of "21." In order to win at Blackjack, you must be free to press bets at certain points of the game as winning streaks appear. Now please realize the importance of knowing when a trend is under way. And also take into consideration the other techniques a player must use when a winning sequence is in process. When the trend you have been waiting for finally appears, you must have the freedom to double up and press bets quickly if you expect to win big. Card counting or the high/low method may be all right when betting nickels and dimes, but you can never rely on the fall of the cards. When you have a large stack bet, the pressure will be at a high level, and you certainly do not want to be guessing and taking unnecessary hits. When that big bet is in front of you, you are forced into playing a hit-and-miss system. The fear of the 10-count card will get in your way, and you simply won't have the nerve to make a proper decision. A reversal of the 10-count card fear is when a card counter is expecting a low-count card and takes the unnecessary hit mentioned earlier, but to his disappointment busts his hand. The times are countless that I've watched card counters double down against the dealer's 10-count card or Ace and, to their dismay, catch a deuce or 3 as their reward for their previous winning formula. On top of all this, there's an additional glitch in the total confusion of the card-counting method: The management, and what they may do in the middle of your winning trend. What has been done in certain casinos in the past is to change the deck or dealers right in the middle of a lucky streak. At certain casinos where a shoe is used, the new dealer simply burned (buried) a card, changing the sequence of the winning trend. But let's suppose none of the above is done and you win a few more hands. Another house procedure is something I have faced in the past, which is a *house shill*. This additional player receives an extra hand, which undoubtedly will change the sequence of your winning trend. Let's go a step further and assume your luck holds. This time you may find that same shill suddenly walking away from your table, changing the card sequence once again. After this, what if a person pretending he's drunk walks up to your table and spills a beer on the playing cards? This has happened to me in the past and it closed the table down completely, leaving me with no guarantee of a lucky sequence. If you continue to win at other tables? Let me just put it simply and firmly, because that's exactly how they'll put it to you. If you're the one player that is not wanted in that particular casino, this is what can be expected next—and please don't laugh. The casino reserves the right (by law) to simply ask you to cash in, and then, commotion or not, have security escort you to the door. And to top it all off, read you a complete set of their own rights!

These warnings about card counting aside, I have always been a strong believer that a player should be completely aware of all cards that have been dealt. My rule is to always keep track of 10-count cards and Aces.

Over the years, I have watched card counting by multitudes of gamblers. After reading some of their systems, I'm sure you will agree that they are confusing and sometimes silly.

One way is by using your chips to count the cards. A card counter using this particular system will be glad to explain that the silver, red, green, and other colors, are usually enough for a player to count cards. But only when pretending he is playing with the chips as he stacks or arranges them.

Also, two or more gamblers playing together, especially if they speak more than one language, can make card counting easier.

Another method is using Morse Code on the back of a Keno ticket and pretending that you're crazy, as you scribble different card counts. If a person does all this, he doesn't have to pretend that he's crazy.

If you think all this is childish, I've heard of people who are good at counting (with a lot of practice, of course) by using their fingers and even their toes, believe it or not.

I have also seen two or more ladies count cards by using different colors of fingernail polish or multi-colored beaded necklaces.

There really is no limit as to how many methods can be used for card counting. I believe at this point I'll leave it up to you to devise your own ways to count cards. But please don't come up with one like painting your teeth different colors, because by doing that you won't be able to smile much; or should I say you'd have to smile all the time.

The Way Blackjack Should Be Played

Ninety-nine percent of the time, I stick to the rules previously mentioned. Those rules and guidelines are logically and mathematically figured to keep the house edge to a fine fraction. You will find that if you play Blackjack the same way, along with total concentration and money management skills, even this game can pay off enough to make it worth the effort.

Usually I try to choose an un-patronized table or reserve one for myself if I play for high stakes. This way I can play single-handedly against the dealer.

There are many techniques in playing Blackjack and the playing systems should be varied. Suppose one keeps getting bad hands. What I would normally do is switch the card I was dealt first and place it on top of the card I was dealt second. Even the placement of one card can make a difference in the sequence of the next shuffle. So if you keep doing this until you begin to get good hands, you've come out ahead. Talking is also important, especially when your dealer is running hot. This can modify the shuffle function, as his own concentration will be interrupted. I have known dealers who told me that because of unlucky streaks, their working hours have been cut. Others have mentioned job loss because too many players were winning.

A dealer's facial features can usually say a great deal on their own. When a dealer is running cold and he's busting, do not talk to him at all. Again, when he's running hot, watch who does the cutting of the cards. When a dealer runs hot because of a particular card cutter (another player at your table), he may offer the cards to be cut by the same player simply because he is cutting the dealer good hands. Conceivably, if this situation arises, don't be afraid to speak up and say, "I believe it's my turn to cut the cards this time." When he's shuffling, as his hands are working constantly, you can get him to change the structure of the shuffle if you try to get his attention by asking a question. A perfect question is what are the most times he has ever busted in a row during his working time. Anything oblique, to get him out of a winning frame.

Here are a few tricks used by a player nicknamed Happy, who loved to drive dealers, in his own phrasing, "out of their minds." If you're a smoker, pretend that your cigarette slipped off the ashtray and let some ashes fall on the table. This will stop the dealer in the middle of his shuffle because he will have to wipe the ashes away to make sure they don't mark a spot on the cards. If that doesn't work, what Happy used to do is light a cigar. This act, plus the smoke from the cigar (Happy figured) would change the shuffle and might even get rid of a player or two. With a few players absent, you can be assured of a change in sequences. "All this may sound rude," Happy said. "But here we're speaking of changing the sequences of the cards!"

If you try any of the above, card sequences had better turn around in your favor—or else it's definitely time to get up from that table and take a walk. Without doubt, you've tried everything, and I hope you were betting the house's minimum. All your attempts could have cost you a stack of chips only to prove something to a dealer or to have a little fun.

When you play Blackjack at a steady pace for a long period, several of the players at your table will have gotten up and walked away. The reason they leave is irrelevant. But what is tremendously important is that new players come to your table and others leave. Undoubtedly, with all this in-and-out traffic, the patterns of card sequences will be altered significantly. Sometimes this can work for the player, but unfortunately many times these changes will be for the worse. This annoyance is to be expected, since it's rare for the same players to remain at a particular table for any length of time. So, when betting high and a large bet is at risk, if a player either arrives or departs, your bet should be decided with great consideration. Since your luck has been good, it may be a good idea for you to politely ask newcomers if they would not get into the game until you played one more hand.

It was a bit after four o'clock in the morning once, when a nice couple approached my table. They walked up at the time when I was experiencing the pleasure of a winning sequence. The couple was extremely polite and fulfilled my request by staying out of the game until I had lost one hand. They stood behind me and cheered every hand I won. They watched me press my bets to the house limit. It was $14,000-plus that the entertained couple watched me win from a stony-faced dealer who had just come on duty.

The Blackjack Wanderer

Some people wander around casinos looking for a winning table. They are usually very cautious, as they first wait to make sure the dealer busts several times. Then, hoping that they will join this happy group, they proceed to play. This method has probably worked for them a few times at Craps. However, the sad part of the plan is that they are innocent of the harm that can be caused by walking in and out of games, unless it's done during the shuffle. By joining a game such as this one, the additional hand will work against the other payers who were previously winning. Most commonly, all this shifting around in and out of tables without respect for other players' well-being, I believe, is unnecessary and nothing but rude. If anything, it's the exact opposite of what most players should be doing. I hope by now readers understand what sequences mean and what happens when more or fewer hands are suddenly involved.

I have good advice for this type of observer. The only way I can find admiration for him is if he walks up to a table when a dealer is running hot and takes a seat. He should sit in the corner chair to the extreme right of the dealer. By taking this position, he would be receiving some of the Aces and pictures that could have been dealt to the dealer's hand. He would surely change the sequence of the cards that the dealer was to receive. This move would not hurt any of the previously losing players. If he was to make such a great move, and he won a lot of money, he could be satisfied that he had made the right choice. But let's carry the situation a bit further, by supposing the dealer got hot again and won two or three hands. Now, to give his scheme another chance, if space allows he plays two hands. This additional hand could change the dealer's winning trend once again. If the sequence of the cards continues to be stubborn and the dealer keeps winning, it's best to stay out of the deal altogether and reenter later. By now, all this in-and-out shifting has undoubtedly given one heck of a jolt to the winning sequence the dealer had been enjoying. Furthermore, a smart player like this one can now be cheered by and perhaps receive congratulations from the other players who are now indebted to him.

Suppose you had a friend, husband, wife, or whomever you'd like to choose as your own personal shill versus the dealer. Then, let's assume this person was to do all the tricks I mentioned, but only betting the minimum. Then, while your shill is protecting your interest, as the cards fall to your advantage you proceed with some very serious betting. Surely, you could be making a killing, but still remain unnoticed. After all, it would be *your friend* who would undoubtedly draw attention. This whole idea may be worth serious thought. Especially when sequences are uneven because, as many of you may already know, winning cards sometimes are just not turning up.

There are casinos that will not let you back in the game once you stay out of a hand. I, personally, contributed a great deal toward the establishment of this rule. There is one thing you should be aware of: They can't stop you from taking a walk and then returning, can they?

Betting Procedures

There are a few more rules for managing your money. Suppose you enter the game with $50. If you're betting $5 per hand, never double the size of your bet until you're ahead $20. If you double your bet this time and you lose the next hand, you're still $10 ahead. If you win again, push your bet up from $10 to $15. If you win that hand, press it up again to $25. Now, stay at that level three more winning hands. After that, you must go up to $50, and if you win, press your bet up to $100 and stay at that betting level until you lose one hand. After losing that bet, you must try one hand at $25. If you lose that hand, try another bet for $25. If you begin to win again, keep adding to your wagers as noted. But if you lose the second $25 hand, it's time to drop your bets down to the $5 minimum until you experience daylight once again. When you're starting to lose, instead of playing one hand, try your luck with two hands for a couple of bets. If this doesn't work, stay out for a short period. Remember, do anything to change the sequence in which the cards are falling. This, you'll notice, won't make your dealer happy. Obviously, when your dealer is unhappy, you must be on the right track. When you first sat down at that table, you didn't sign any contract to play each and every hand. Never stay at a table where you keep getting bad hands, or if you begin to lose a sequence of two or three bets twice in a row. The cards are obviously falling against you, and you should stop playing at that table.

When you're on a winning streak, if the cards or dealers are replaced, drop your bet down to the minimum until you see how the cards fall. If you're not known in the casino, and you win a couple of hundred dollars, it may not be a bad idea to tip the dealer or make a bet for him on your hand. This will keep dealers from reshuffling too often. But don't ever believe that, just because you tipped, the pit boss doesn't know you're winning.

With four or six decks in the shoe, a new dealer in some places will burn a card before dealing, which could be in the middle of a winning trend. That's when a person should call the Gaming Control

Board and see how they respond. With a single deck, a new dealer must reshuffle, using his own method. Always remember, when you're winning you will become a popular figure. Casino executives keep their eyes on you, whether you know it or not.

Sometimes the odds can drop to $^{50}/_{50}$. And the way the cards fall can change drastically, either in your favor or to the house's advantage. But let's stick to $^{50}/_{50}$ for the time being. You may flip a coin and it turns up heads 20 consecutive times, but on the 21st flip of that same coin the odds of it coming up heads are still $^{50}/_{50}$. The odds are not 20 to 1, as some players tend to think. Therefore, throughout the time you're playing, don't forget that you're aiming for that one winning streak. When it finally appears, you must back it with your chips if you're aiming for a heavy win. It's depressing, indeed, to watch someone win twenty consecutive hands and win a measly $100 at $5 per bet.

Suppose you won $500 betting this way and you keep winning more hands than you're losing. You should advance your bets, at $25 minimum, and keep it at that level until you lose $100. If that happens, it's time to drop back to the $5 minimum once again. If you lose $50 at $5 per bet, it's time to get up and forget about that table. You can always find another, and begin with the original $50. However, if you win another $1,000 betting this way at several different tables, it's time to raise your minimum bet to $50 and buy $500 worth of chips at each table. If you keep winning with the $50 bets, press bets accordingly. But if the cards turn against you, it's time to drop your betting action to the $5 minimum once again. Also, if you lose $200 at four different tables, it's time to go back home and try it all over again on another trip, from your $1,300 win.

When you play Blackjack and find one table where you continue to win, never leave it until you sense that the streak is over. You should never walk away and leave a winning table, to swim in the pool or to take a nap, and expect to find the same card sequence when you return.

The odds of 100 coin tosses according to the science of probabilities have an expectancy of 50 heads and 50 tails. However, there is no guarantee in what sequence the 100 tosses will appear. On every 100 coin tosses, the sequence of heads and tails will be different. This is what a player always counts on, he stops when the cards fall against him and he bets high when they're falling in his favor.

If you're a beginner and unless you are very wealthy, never bring more than $500 with you for a gambling stake. You can always be a high roller on the casino's money after you sense how your luck is going. Always remember, you can win a million from a $2 bet if luck is meant to go in that direction. But unfortunately, a player can also lose a million chasing a $2 bet. When losing, never chase losses by pouring out more money. That's the major key in separating the winners from the losers. A gambling stake is to be used only for sampling your luck and nothing more. If you are a winner, good luck will force you to bet higher. Never double a bet when you're losing. Usually, that's the first step to total catastrophe. If you break these rules, from that point on you'll find yourself facing a different destiny.

Once I was taking the action on Blackjack (in a private game) being the Bank, with thousands in front of me. There were several losers playing during the two-day period the game lasted. Two of the players quit the game. Their system had been to double up as they lost. Despite my warnings, they continued using what gamblers call "The Old Martingale System,"* telling me how they would surely break me. Less than an hour into their system, their plan had culminated in its usual failure.

"I hear you give lessons on Blackjack," one of my Greek opponents said, grinning. "I heard this rumor from a Las Vegas pit boss!"

"You're a walking contradiction!" I answered as I put the deck down, giving everyone at the table a break. "If I remember right, only thirty minutes ago you were the one who was giving all the

---

*The "Martingale System" is the doubling of bets until a hand is won, then returning to the size of an original wager.

lessons."

The opposite of doubling up as you lose is to double every time you win. At times, premature pressing can be costly if there are no long winning sequences. When the wins and losses are chopping back and forth, you can actually lose unnecessarily, without realizing it. Below, a quick study of the wins and losses shows the outcome of pressing your bets each time you win a hand. Pressing your bet each time you win indicates that you end up losing double the size of your bet on the next hand. When there is no immediate winning trend, you can actually lose money. This is why a player is much better off not pressing his bet until he has won four consecutive hands. Then, if he loses that bet, he still has a profit to show from the whole transaction.

W	L	W	I.	W	L	W	I.	W	L
+1	−2	−1	−3	−2	−4	−3	−5	−4	6
1	2	3	4	5	6	7	8	9	10

If you had not pressed your bets, instead of the minus 6 result you would be at even money after ten hands had been played. So when the wins and losses are chopping back and forth, you actually end up beating yourself when doubling up every time you win a hand. This type of play I've called "premature pressing." This is why sometimes if you're winning more hands than you're losing (without a sequence, of say, ten or fifteen wins in a row), you may be much better off not pressing your bets as you win, but to bet with larger size units. For instance, instead of betting $5, bet $25 per hand if you're winning more bets than you're losing. (This method should apply also when playing Craps, Baccarat, or any game similar to a coin toss.)

Chapter 10

Baccarat

At this game the bettor may bet either on the Bank or the Player side. The structure of play in Baccarat is always predetermined by the rules. Therefore, as a standard procedure, the bettor has no choice other than on which side to bet his money.

When betting the Bank you have an edge over the Player of 1.36 percent. However, when you bet the Bank and win, you are automatically charged 5 percent of the total wager made. This will calculate to a 1.17 percent disadvantage for the player betting on the Bank. In addition, something else to consider is that as you continue to win on the Bank and press your bets, you also contribute to the casino cut, which is the 5 percent juice. This drain in a period of a few hours can mount to hundreds or even thousands of dollars, depending on the size of wagers. That's when the cut can prove hazardous to your stake. Throughout a big bettor's lifetime, he or she has paid hundreds and perhaps thousands of dollars in juice alone at Baccarat.

When betting on the Player, you don't pay the juice as you win, but you're always the underdog by the above mentioned 1.36 percent, or *hidden* house advantage. The odds are unchanging. All casinos must have an edge to cover their enormous expenses.

A perfect example of the need for profit, is the so-called *tie bet*. This bet is made before the cards are dealt. The casino rule on the tie bet is that the count of the cards dealt on both sides—the Bank and the Player—will add up to a total count of equal value after the

108

deal is over. The house cut on this bet—even though the payoff is 9 for 1, which is reality equals 8 to 1—carries a staggering 14.1 percent house profit.

At Baccarat, pictures or any 10-count cards, which may consist of one or more cards, equal zero. The highest winning hand is a 9 or any cards drawn that add up to 9. The lowest winning hand is a 1 or any cards drawn which add up to a 1. For instance, a 4 and 7 equals a total of just 1. A 5 and a 7 equals a total of only 2. A 6 and a 7 equals a diminished total of 3, etc. Again, any 10-count or any of two or three cards which add up to a total of 10 equal zero, which is the lowest count. This game is simple to understand. Dealers at Baccarat must call the card counts accurately, as cards are drawn. Therefore, no mistakes are permitted during the playing. To most players who have never played this game, it may appear difficult to understand. However, a short session at a table will simplify things.

When playing, I try to plot the structure of card sequences. As in other right or wrong two-sided games, the wins of either Bank or Player are similar to the coin tosses previously noted. One way to play the game is by choosing to bet low when you're losing and high when you're winning. Money management remains the winning key. Since Baccarat is dealt out of a shoe, which consists of eight decks, there will be times when the cards will run hot for Bank, and other times hot for Player. The difficult task, of course, is to determine the sequence in advance. If you try to outguess the fall of cards, you may expect to lose in the long run. There is, however, a way to bet Bank or Player and catch sequences which may occur on one or even on both sides. Experienced players call this "following the shoe." If the shoe runs hot for either side, you'll win big as long as you increase bets when you're winning. The way to bet this method is by betting one side and staying there until that side loses. Then switch to the side that won last. If the wins chop back and forth, you will lose every bet you wager. But two or more wins, either on Bank or on Player, will bring a profit. The explanation is quite simple. The wins will have to chop back and forth consistently in order for you to lose a large sum of money. A different interpretation is that since the cards have no plans of their own, the majority of the time the wins will not chop back and forth. A consistent chop of wins rarely occurs. However, short or long sequences are common. For this method to succeed, I recommend that you begin the play with at least twenty units. Then, patience is required to reach your goal, which is to spot a sequence and press your bets, winning as much as possible for the short time the trend lasts. A winning sequence is a gambler's passport to the Heavenly gates. At times the wins can run hot on both sides, Bank or Player. As in Blackjack, a Baccarat shoe of eight decks can run extremely streaky. Thus, when stubborn streaks are underway, your betting action must follow the trend and the size of your wagers must progress with the trend. Each winning sequence will bring in chips to make up for losing sessions. In addition, only your *losing plateaus* should be considered. A winner has no plateau limitations when he's running hot. When I bet the follow the shoe method, no matter if Player or Bank wins, I always show a profit. I have won $10,000 or $20,000 in a matter of moments, from a single winning sequence dealt out of the shoe.

During winning sequences, you must also be cautious. As the cards are being dealt out of the shoe, no card should be dealt out of sequence to any other player or house shill. If a card is accidentally dealt out of turn, that particular card must not be burned. One card dealt out of sequence and the structure of the play will change. This happened to me many years ago. My bet had mounted to the house limit. When I complained, my bet was returned to me, but since the card had been burnt, the winning sequence ended right after the innocent mistake was made by the shill.

Baccarat was first played in Las Vegas during the late 1950s. The game originally offered was the European Chemin de Fer version, but a short time later it became the game we now know. The semi-secluded rooms in which the game is played in most casinos have special table limits. The minimum is also different from that of the other games offered. Special value chips are used, usually worth $20, which is the minimum wager permitted at most games. Recently, some casinos have hiked up the minimum bet to $100. The house limit has also been raised to a much higher level. At the original MGM Grand, Mini Baccarat was made available and could be played at $5 per bet. (This was back in the 1970s, however, and this resort also offered a high-stake Baccarat game.)

Chapter 11

The Most Effective
Craps Systems

Betting the Don't Pass and the Don't Come has advantages which do not exist on the Pass and Come lines. Since 1965 I have won and lost millions of dollars thus, being a Don't bettor is not a decision I came to by accident, habit, or superstition. Backing the Don't side of the table has choices which, if taken advantage of at the right time, can turn the odds in your favor. However, there have been times when the dice were passing and the shooters were repeating numbers between comeout sevens. Sometimes this can occur, as the dice do not always fall mathematically as they should, and I have switched to the Pass and Come side of the table on occasion. During those few times, I discovered that it was difficult to press any winning trend. I don't like to think that there are too many players who, when winning, press their bets any quicker than I do, but betting on the Pass and Come lines is sometimes daunting for me. Since I have won so consistently on the Don't, a certain fear has developed regarding the old number 7. A simple division of 6 into 36 will explain just how often a 7 is thrown. This occurrence has been repeated countless times against the chips of millions of gamblers for decades. Still, gamblers choose to ignore this fact, attempting to overcome this proven law of mathematics.

The 7 is the key factor in Craps and, years ago, dealers heard me define that number, which consists of six combinations. The Pass and

Come player is betting that the dice will completely forget that, mathematically, the 7 must show up an average of 6 times in 36 tosses. At the same time he is hoping that the 7 will show up only on the comeout roll, when he needs it. He is also asking for the 7 to come up repeatedly, regardless of the 30 other combinations. And for the 7 not to show up at all until he makes various points many times over. This is why he is in need of great good luck. Asking for those miracles to happen consistently is one hell of a wish. If someone wants to convince me how complicated Craps can become, all he has to do is mention the Pass and Come Lines. When I bet, I want to do so with some logical reason behind my wagers. The Don't Pass bettor is asking for any of 30 combinations to show up just once, prior to the six-way number 7. After a point is thrown he is asking for the 7 to appear, once only, before the point, any of 4, 5, 6, 8, 9, or 10, is matched. In reality, after a point has been established, the 7, which has the most combinations, has become the Don't Pass bettors point each time the dice are tossed.

The Don't Come bettor is asking for the 7 to come up once every six rolls, which is mathematically reasonable. Even when dice go crazy and a total of twelve numbers, any of 4, 5, 6, 8, 9, or 10, is tossed, he can still break even. Please keep in mind that any time you toss the dice more than six rolls without a 7 showing up, you should consider that roll a significantly long one indeed. Each time a player places a bet on the Pass or Come line, the casino is automatically betting the Don't side. I hope this time I have convinced you that the Don't side is your most logical bet.

If you've played Craps for many years you have probably occasionally witnessed this flipping of the dice. Over the years I have observed that in a substantial number of tosses the dice have a tendency to flip to the opposite side of the combination which was in front of the shooter prior to the toss. The next throw would frequently fall to the opposite sides when the shooter picked up the dice the exact way the stickman had turned them over to him. This flipping usually works against the Don't Pass and Don't Come bettor. The dealer's turning of the dice may appear a matter of chance to someone with little experience. However, the players who are well versed in casino Craps and understand the various combinations of the dice are familiar with this particular method used against the Don't bettor. Thus, if the point is a 4, the stickman serves the dice with the 10 on top, opposite the 4. Similar tactics can be used against all bets on the Don't Pass and Don't Come. In explanation, the numbers 4 and 10 are opposite each other. The 5 and 9 are opposite each other. The 6 and 8 are also opposite each other. Ace-deuce is opposite 11, etc. Most important is that a 7 is always opposite another 7.

It is standard for the shooter to shake the dice repeatedly before making the toss. He is also allowed brief trial mini-tosses by arranging combinations to his liking. When he has the desired combination, he is required to hit the opposite wall of the table. (Stickmen gently admonish lady shooters whose tosses land short of the wall.) This may result in either a point being made, another number, or a 7 out. One way for a Pass line shooter to possibly turn the odds in his favor is by turning the dice to the *opposite* side of his point. The Don't bettor and shooter should turn the dice to the *exact* side. When betting the Don't Come, a sensible number to pick up and throw is always a 7, but only after two or three points have been established.

When approaching a table the shooter should first acquire an appropriate slot. The most effective location to stand at is one end of the table while shooting to the opposite end. Side locations are not as effective. The straighter the shot you have at the other end of the table, the more this method may pay off. After the desired combination is chosen, the dice should be tossed high, around two and one-half to three feet from the table. The distance is also very important. The dice should land near the opposite side of the table, only a few inches from the studs. Then the dice will bounce and flip, and, more often than the odds indicate, could land on the opposite side of the combination prior to the toss. After a lot of practice, a certain skill or English can be acquired, and the results can be rewarding.

When betting the Don't side, a player may throw the dice if he chooses. On one occasion I walked up to a table, where I was the sole player, and bought chips. As the dice were offered to me I made a bet on the Don't Pass. The stickman mumbled a comment to the other dealers.

"What's he trying to prove?" he asked.

Then the shift boss walked up. "That's like committing suicide!" he laughed. "Are you sure you want to shoot betting on the Don't?"

"I'll make a deal with both of you," I answered. "Ask the dice the same question. If they answer you, I'll take your advice. I'll assume you're right. In the meantime, hold back on your commentary."

Every Craps shooter ought to learn dice combinations. In fact, it would be best if he make it his business, just like a stickman, to memorize them. If he wishes to switch combinations when playing, he should learn to do this quickly, because if he decides to turn dice in a casino, the boxman will usually ask him to hurry up. Let's suppose a shooter throws a 4. Two turns forward or backwards on the layout with his palm can quickly turn the dice to the opposite side of the 4, which is the 10. The same simple procedure can be applied to any of the other combinations when attempting to locate the exact opposite point, prior to the toss. Depending on the combination the stickman serves, only one die will require a quick adjustment by a simple turn.

Moving on, certain procedures will prove helpful, and will assist you in properly handling your wagers. Assume you have $100 on the Don't Pass and the shooter rolls a 10. You now have $100 no 10. Suppose you take another $100 and tell the dealer to place it on the 10. Let's examine what you've done. If the shooter repeats his 10 you lose $100 on the Don't Pass. But at the same time you collect $180 plus your own $100—from placing the 10—equaling an $80 net profit. On the other hand, if the shooter rolls a 7, your $100 place bet would be picked up, but you would collect $100 on the Don't Pass–no 10 bet. A similar situation can be achieved on any established Don't Pass or Don't Come point, and thereafter a near-equal amount of money is placed on that particular number, which might be any 4, 5, 6, 8, 9, or 10. Something else to remember is to tell the payoff man to put the working button on your place bet each time this transaction is taking place. (The purpose for this request is explained in detail later in this chapter.)

Another way to insure your bets is by standing on one side of the table and betting $100 Don't Pass and $100 Don't Come on every roll after that. At the same time, across from you, a friend is betting $50 to Pass and $50 to Come, plus taking $50 odds on those numbers for every following roll until the shooter sevens out and the roll is over. Let's go back one more time and examine what can be accomplished with this system. If the roll is a long one, while you're breaking even between your Don't and Come bets, for every number that's repeated your friend collects odds on that Come bet. Meanwhile, you've insured your bets from the Don't side. In addition, if the shooter repeats his Pass line point, and right after that he tosses a 7 on the comeout roll—while the numbers are loaded with bets—down come the odds to your friend from all the Come bets. (After the Pass Line point is repeated and the next number tossed is a 7, by casino rule the payoff man must bring back the odds from any Come bets previously made to that Pass and Come bettor. The odds on all Come bets are returned. Only the original bet, prior to taking odds, is lost. This rule holds true only for the Come bets, and does not pertain to the Pass Line bets). As a result, only $50 is picked up from each of the Come bets, while you are paid *full win* $100 on all your Don't Come bets. Casinos pay true odds on all Come line bets, the same as they do on the Pass line. When you are winning, odds collected on the Pass and Come lines are 2 to 1 on the 4 or 10; 3 to 2 on the 5 or 9; and 6 to 5 on the 6 or 8. The above way to bet is called the right and wrong method. It is an interesting method to learn from, but if you bet that way consistently, caution is advised. If you are at a table where too many 7s are tossed and the rolls are short ones, you're losing $100 on the Don't side but only receiving $50 on the Come. One thousand sevens, at $50 a pop, and that's $50,000 that all the repeat numbers, etc., will have to account for. The only way this system will pay off is if the dice are repeating many numbers between 7s. One thing that's important to remember is that your bets are insured; thus you will not lose all your bets at the same time as you would by betting the Come line only. During that period you do not need to be concerned about the 11s, because ace-deuce makes up the difference, plus you have the double-aces on your side as an extra bonus.

For decades casinos have had odds of all games figured to the fraction. Also, calculations on most betting variations in Craps have assured casino bosses that no method exists to reverse the minus percentage offered. Otherwise, the game would either cease, or necessary changes of the rules would have to be effected. As mentioned before, no casino game can pay true odds because of the huge expenses that casinos run up daily. To explain further, I believe casino operators will not modify current rules unless large losses have been perceived. But some casinos lost big money to some customers before certain regulations were changed. The fact is that statisticians and computers can only come up with facts and figures after a problem has been accurately pinpointed. Thus, experts neglected to enter all the possible maneuvers into their computers simply because all the facts had not yet been discovered about the game.

Suppose you bet $22 on the Don't Pass and the shooter rolls a 4. The next move you should make is to place the inside numbers 5, 6, 8, 9 for $22 across. As the shooter continues, suppose he rolls an 8? You take down your place bet on the 8 along with your profit. Then he rolls a 6, and you also take down the 6 along with the profit. So far you have brought down $13 from the 8 and $13 from the 6, equalling $26. The total profit is $14. Your next move is to ask the payoff man to bring down your 5 and 9 place bets, equalling $10. Then you wait till the shooter hits your 4 or most likely sevens out. The odds are 2 to 1 that he will seven out. If the 4 is not made you will be ahead a total of $36. At this point, the question to ask is how many times will a shooter throw a 4 back-to-back or seven out with no tosses in between. This system is designed for the player who believes on *placing* numbers, but has lost money consistently through the years because of hitting the 7 right after the comeout roll. Insuring your place bets, by first making a Don't Pass wager, is what allows you to place the *inside* numbers without fear of a 7. The more difficult the number is to repeat, as are 4 or 10, the more insurance you acquire on your *place* bets that follow. During certain *long rolls*, you may find it very tempting to leave your place bets for one more roll or longer. But that's when the odds on the 7 increase and the loss of those bets is to be expected. Whenever the Don't Pass numbers 4 or 10 are repeated back-to-back, or prior to bringing your place bets down, my advice is that you should wait for the next shooter and start over. If the Don't Pass number is 6 or 8, however, you may still follow through with the above method or let the 6 or 8 play. There is an additional method to insure the 6 or 8, and that's by *placing* either number for $24. If it is repeated, the payoff will be $28. The original bet made on the Don't Pass should be figured, in advance, to equal the nearest even dollar payoff on the bet placed later. The 5 or 9 Don't Pass number is to be handled the same as the 4 and 10. Another important procedure to follow each time your place bets are combined with a Don't bet is to ask the payoff man to put the working button on your place bets.

The house cut when you're *placing* the number is not as low as the .591 rate when betting the Don't Pass and Don't Come and laying double odds. I must alert you that when *placing* the 6 or 8, the house p.c. is 1.51 percent. When *placing* the 5 or 9, it's 4 percent. However, when *placing* the 4 or 10, the p.c. increases to 6.67 percent. Casino rule allows you to "buy" the 4 or 10—in advance—at a cost of 5 percent.

Nectar—The Real Juice

A flat bet is a wager that does not include odds. This term is used to identify a bet that is separate from one which includes the combination of an original bet with odds.

How to pick up a flat bet on the Don't Pass and Don't Come without fearing the 7 has always been a puzzle. If I could discover the answer to this problem I would then have an edge on the game. The trouble was that I was only investigating the Don't Pass bet. However, after I combined this move with the Don't Come a solution seemed at hand.

Let's assume that you have a bet on the Don't Pass for $100 and the point is 8. Then you lay $240 against the 8—provided that you are at a casino allowing double odds (which most do). The next bet that you make is a flat Don't Come for $300. Now, suppose a 10 is rolled. The next proper move is to *lift the odds* $240 off the Don't Pass number, the *no* 8. This leaves you with $100 *no* 8 and $300 *no* 10. If the 7 was to show up right after the 8 you would break even. The dealer would pick up your $300 flat bet on the Don't Come, but he would have to pay you $300 on the Don't Pass *no* 8 because it was not made. During this one important toss—which is the second toss—the $100 *no* 8 and the $240 odds you layed next to the original bet are insuring your $300 Don't Come flat bet. On the other hand, if the 7 doesn't show on the second toss, you are left with $100 *no* 8 and $300 *no* 10. This results in a 6 to 5 advantage on the *no* 8 bet and 2 to 1 edge for your second bet, *no* 10. The total amount you collect from your Don't Pass bet equals the lump sum on the Don't Come flat bet, insuring the second bet for one critical roll. In addition, the second bet—the flat Don't Come bet—insures the Don't Pass bet for that one critical toss. If the dice go really crazy and the 8 is tossed back-to-back you would still have an additional $300 *no* 8 to be repeated on the Don't Come.

This system works much better and you'll have the best results when wagering at tables accepting 10 times odds. With 10 times odds you can accomplish all the above with the result of a much bigger flat bet on the Don't Come.

Let's say you are at a casino which accepts 10 times odds and you make a $100 bet on the Don't Pass. Now, assume that the first number tossed is again an 8. You can now lay up to $1,200 against the 8. Your next bet should be a flat bet of $1,100 on the Don't Come. If the following throw is a 10—or a 4, 5, 6, 8, or 9—you have a definite edge. For now let's stick to having $1,300 *no* 8 and $1,100 *no* 10. To simplify matters you immediately lift the $1,200 lay against the 8. At this point you have a 6 to 5 edge on your *no* 8, which is your Don't Pass bet. You also have a 2 to 1 advantage on your *no* 10 Don't Come bet. (We must go back to understand an additional option. If the second number—the Don't Come number—is either a 6 or 8 and you do not wish to let it play, you may make an additional Don't Come bet for an equal amount, hoping to pick up a tougher number like a 4, 5, 9, or 10). If the next roll is any of those numbers which are not repeated as frequently you should now place the *no* 6 or *no* 8— which is the second bet—for an equal amount *place bet* while letting the second Don't Come bet work. (All this may be difficult to understand. But if you use dice and some playing chips or even beans at home while testing the foregoing example for half an hour, the procedures will become much clearer.) However, if the first number is any of 4, 5, 9, or 10, you let it play. The number to repeat, in this case, is a tough one and there is no reason for a second Don't Come bet. You should make additional bets on the Don't Come after either a 6 or an 8, which are frequent repeat points. The second or third bet, where you may lay odds against the previous number for one roll only and then pick up the odds, is to obtain a tougher point to match. As mentioned, the numbers that most rarely appear are 4, 5, 9, and 10. Thus, to attempt and achieve more advantageous points, you follow through with either or both of the above procedures. Regardless how you choose your play, all you're attempting to do is ditch the 7 for one roll. Once you escape the dangerous come-out number, 7, you have an edge on the Don't side. It pays to remember that, for many decades, casinos have profited from barring the double-six and by offering payoffs which differ slightly from the true odds. If a player manages to have the odds on his side, even by a fraction of a percentage, and follows strict money management rules, he is bound to come out a winner. All he or she needs to do is play for long sessions and carefully follow our various instructions.

Some of the ways to bet will seem new and, to some degree, difficult to understand. My advice is that you study carefully the format of each wagering pattern. Before betting this way you should try a test run with at least 1,000 samplings or tosses of the dice. Please don't drive, fly, or run to the nearest casino believing you'll break the bank. Always remember that the casino odds, which clearly present a minus expectancy, are always the same and never change. The method you choose and the way you use your money during your gaming session are precisely what can bend the odds and allow you to win. At certain instances you may enjoy up to a 2-to-1 advantage over the casino. But don't misconstrue the facts by assuming you have a 2-to-1 edge before you make a single bet. As you continue betting on the Don't side, other opportunities will arise.

At first, bet $5 on the Don't Pass. If the shooter throws any of these inside numbers, 5, 6, 8, or 9, lay 10 times odds against it. So let's assume that someone rolls an 8 and you have a $5 bet on the Don't Pass. You lay $60 odds against the 8 for the next roll. Your next action is to bet $55 *flat* on the Don't Come. Now, say the next number tossed is a 4. You pick up the $60 odds you layed against the 8. This move simplifies matters, leaving you with $5 *no* 8 and $55 flat bet *no* 4 on the backline. The idea is to have a flat bet without fearing the 7. After the flat bet has been established you automatically have a marginal edge over the casino. The reason you lay 10 times odds against the 8 is to protect the $55 bet you follow up with on the Don't Come for that one roll only. The amount you would collect on the Don't Pass should equal the total flat bet wagered on the Don't Come. Thus, those two bets on the Don't Pass are insuring the *flat* bet on the Don't Come—against the 7—during the second toss of the dice. If the 8 is repeated back-to-back, you still have $55 *no* 8 on the Don't Come. Most likely, this bet will not be repeated, because the shooter would have to throw three 8s in a row before a 7 is tossed. If you so desire, you may follow up with a third bet, which would be a second Don't Come bet for $55. If a 4, 5, 9, or 10 is tossed, you should place the *no* 8 for $54 and let the new Don't Come number play. If the *no* 8 repeats, you collect $63 from your place bet. Again, each time a place bet is made, you must ask the payoff man to activate the working button by placing it on your $54 place bet. Suppose that the next time he comes out, the shooter rolls a 9. After already having bet $5 on the Don't Pass, you will now lay $60 against the 9 and, at the same time, bet $45 *flat* on the Don't Come. Since you would collect 2 to 3 for your *no* 9 bet, the amount of your flat bet must change. Thus, since the total amount you would collect if a 7 is tossed next is $45 on the Don't Pass, the total amount of your flat bet on the Don't Come should also be $45.

Any 5, 6, 8, or 9 are good numbers to lay odds on the Don't Pass and then follow up with the other moves on the Don't Come. However, if the Don't Pass number is a 4 or 10, it is not as wise to follow through with the rest of the transactions. The reason for this is that you can lay up to $100 against the 4 or 10 from an original $5 Don't Pass bet. Also, because your Don't Come bet—the total flat bet of $55—would not insure the full $105 on the Don't Pass. Meanwhile, if you were to get hit with a 4 or 10 back-to-back, you'd lose $105 on the Don't Pass while insuring only $55 on the Don't Come. If the Don't Pass number is either a 4 or 10 you already have a 2 to 1 advantage over the casino. The best time to bet this method is when the Don't Pass number is 6 or 8. But this can become a long, drawn-out situation. My recommendation is that, in order to speed up the action, you also bet when the Don't Pass number (the original bet) is either a 5 or 9. While betting this method there are additional rules which should be carefully followed and never neglected. If the shooter repeats your second bet, which is your flat bet on the Don't Come, you should never make another bet against that same shooter. Simply wait until he exhausts his roll. This rule will insulate you from long rolls, which can become very expensive. During the session, you'll notice that many times you will either win or lose your second bet—the flat bet on the Don't Come—by an Ace-deuce, two Aces, or an eleven. If you win this bet, pick up your chips. Also, at the same time, pick up the odds from your Don't Pass bet and wait for the next shooter. If you lose with an eleven, accept the loss, pick up the odds from your Don't Pass bet, and wait for the next shooter. Throughout this playing period, your main need is to win one bet. Also, to never lose more than one flat bet to the same shooter.

As you can comprehend, the only time the odds at Craps actually turn in favor of the bettor is when he's betting the Don't Pass and the Don't Come—and it is never otherwise. First, practice at home and make sure you are following correct procedures. Then, when you're betting your method in a casino, if you lose a few bets don't ignore your winning system. Always remember your previous sampling at home. You may lose a few bets, but then break even by winning them back. At least that has been my experience.

During the game make sure the stickman is not turning the dice opposite to your Don't Pass or Don't Come points. If the dice are not brought back to you with the combination that was showing on top after the toss, mention this fact to the pit boss in charge. At certain casinos you may be told that the dice are turned over so the boxman (sitting on a stool in the table's center) can inspect other combinations on the dice. Your answer to that should be that the dice can be turned to the opposite side to be inspected, but after this is accomplished they should be turned right back to the same combination which rolled last. (If a casino pit boss must have the dice inspected after each roll, there is always another casino not too far away.)

When you gamble it's always best to bring a good friend along as an eyewitness. If for some reason there is need to call the Gaming Control Board, have your friend secretly make the call. Depending on the complaint, the Gaming Control Board's representative has the right to review the tape from the camera over the table. If he writes out a report, make sure you ask for a copy. If you have a serious complaint, call an attorney and subpoena the tapes immediately.

Following the Do's and the Don'ts mentioned in this chapter can be the safest method for smart players to gamble. This next method can work at Craps without laying odds.

Suppose you bet $30 on the Don't Pass and you roll an 8. Next, you make a $30 Don't Come bet, but this time you roll a 10. Since the 8 is only a 6-to-5 proposition and can be matched a lot easier than the 10, you place the 8 for $30. As a result, if the 8 repeats you

The 10 Times Odds Method

Don't Pass points recommended to play out the 10 times odds method are any of 5, 6, 8, or 9.	Pick up odds layed on the Don't Pass after the Don't Come flat bet has been established.	Make Don't Come flat bet when the points are any of 5, 6, 8, or 9 on the Don't Pass. Also, after the Don't Come point has been established you have a huge edge over the casino.	Go for second Don't Come flat bet, if desired, when the first Don't Come point is 6 or 8.
When the point is any of 5, 6, 8, or 9, lay 10 times odds.	Always pick up the odds layed—after the Don't Come flat bet has been established. If the second number tossed is any of 7, Ace-deuce, two Aces, or 11, stop betting and lift the odds and payoff from the Don't Pass. Leave the original bet up.	No odds should be layed after this accomplishment. Hopefully the Don't Come flat bet will be any of 4, 5, 9, or 10. Even when it's 6 or 8 you still have a 6 to 5 edge over the casino.	Hopefully the second Don't Come point will be any of 4, 5, 9, or 10.
When the first point is either a 4 or a 10. First bet—or the Don't Pass bet.	No bet is required, although it's optional. Second transaction.	No bet is required. / Second bet, or first Don't Come flat bet.	No bet is required. / Third bet, if desired, or second Don't Come flat bet.

When betting the above method the idea is to either pick up a difficult number to repeat, as any of 4, 5, 9, or 10, and insure the 6 or 8. Also to clinch one flat bet at a time. In addition, if you win or lose a flat bet, wait for the next shooter. After practicing for a few minutes, all purposes will become clear and the transactions elementary.

collect $35. In the meantime you have a 2-to-1 edge over the casino on the *no* 10. If the first number for $30 on the Don't Pass is 4, 5, 9, or 10, you do not make a second bet. But if it's a 6 or 8, you place it for $30 and follow up by making a $30 Don't Come bet. Again, the purpose of the Don't Come bet is to catch a second number which is a more difficult point to match, like the 4, 5, 9, or 10. (If the Don't Come number is a 6 you place it also.)

A reversal of the above is if you make a $30 bet on the Don't Pass and this time you roll a 10. Because the 10 rarely shows back-to-back, you make a Don't Come bet for $30. Your Don't Pass bet, the *no* 10, is insuring your Don't Come bet for one roll against the dangerous number 7. As a result, if the Don't Come number tossed is any of 4, 5, or 9, you let it work. If it's either a 6 or 8, you may still place it for $30.

Another logical bet is to make a Don't Pass wager for $12 when you roll a 10. Then you place the 6 and 8 for $6 each. If either place bet repeats, you collect the profit and ask the payoff man to bring down both of your place bets. You still have $12 *no* 10, which equals a 2-to-1 edge over the house. (The same method can be chosen if the Don't Pass number tossed is a 4.)

The above Do's and Don'ts are different ways to wager, with no guarantee of winning. But by understanding those methods you acquire a much wider view of Craps, allowing you to take advantage of situations which may arise during your time at the table.

Whenever you *place* a bet, which is accompanied by a Don't Pass or Don't Come bet, you must ask the dealer to put the working button on your place bet. This request can be made by saying the word "working" at the same time you make any place bet. Otherwise, after the Don't Pass point is repeated and a 7 is tossed during the comeout roll, according to the house rule the place bets are off on that roll; they are not working. Thus, you would get paid on all your Don't bets, but if any of your place bets were repeated, during the comeout roll, the place bets would be at a standoff or a push. This part can be costly and confusing. But if the simple word "working" is said, the working button means that the comeout counts.

A casino employee may tell you that the method you're betting has been tried for several decades and usually loses. Supposedly there is no allegedly foolproof system that the dealers have not seen in action. One system I did bet was the 10 times odds method. It so happened that I won from the first bet until I grew tired. That was fourteen hours later. Similar performances continued for more than a month. During that time, several observers asked me to explain the rules of the method. My answer was that they should either follow my betting action, or else wait until my book was published.

When betting any of the systems mentioned, you'll note that the action is extremely fast and can sometimes be confusing. As a result, mistakes can be made by the bettor or even the payoff man. This is why a smart player must watch all his bets as well as all payoffs.

Regardless of the methods mentioned in this chapter, there will always be players who will remain dedicated Pass Line bettors. Because of this, I must reveal a betting procedure with slightly different payoff results.

As mentioned before, when betting the Come Line—after the Pass number is repeated and a 7 is tossed—all the odds accompanied by the original Come bets are returned to the bettor. If I was betting the Don't Pass and the Don't Come at the same time, the casino and I would have the same bets. The only difference, and it's a huge difference, is that when the Pass Line number is repeated and then a 7 is tossed, I collect in full on all my wagers and on all the odds I layed. Hence, throughout the session I never give back a red cent to the casinos. Obviously, except for the casino's barring of the double-six, I must have a bigger advantage than the house does against the Come bettor. There is your additional proof that the Don't Come is by far the best investment to bet your money on. If the Pass bettor still doesn't wish to alter his style, there are no real salvations, but there is a grain of information that should be considered. Stay away from the Pass Line entirely and make single bets on the Come-line instead. When betting the Pass Line you are giving the house a clear edge. However, by betting the Come and your Pass Line bet wins and then a 7 is tossed, you certainly have your odds back. Therefore, when considering double and 10 times odds available, logic favors the Come bet over the supposedly "logical" Pass Line proposition. Casinos have a rule that in order to shoot the dice you must have first placed a bet on the front or backline, which is the Pass or Don't Pass Line. If you wish to shoot the dice, you can bet the minimum and still wager a sizeable Come bet. I hope that you have absorbed the essence of how to shave the casino edge to the minimum, and the overall importance of the minus odds expectancy as it accumulates.

Casinos have rules with which many players are unfamiliar. Dealers are aware of all the house rules because their jobs require this knowledge. However, the average tourist is not aware of many of their rules. Thus, in most cases, a newcomer to the tables is at a disadvantage without knowledge of the games. Certain casino instructors are present to teach tourists how to play, but they offer only a simplistic synopsis, just enough to get people involved. Television advice on gambling is available in hotel rooms on specific channels, but it is also brief. Hardly, an educational experience—or a way to spend a honeymoon in a Las Vegas suite. A player should learn all the house rules on his own, and, whenever possible, prosper from them.

When a player runs lucky, he is happy and his hands are busy making bets. His body is warm and his hands have a slight coating of perspiration. The reason for this is that the body is functioning properly, as the adrenal glands are at work, stimulating the heart and the nervous system. When a player's luck runs sour, his behavior reflects it. He is nervous, frustrated, and depressed. He knows that he's losing. He simply cannot get ahead regardless of which game he chooses, and he's aware of this phenomenon. Thus, if a person pays attention to his sensations, combined with the way the cards or dice are falling, there is absolutely no reason not to be aware of his luck's direction. That's when he should occupy himself with anything but gambling. There will be other opportunities when he can win enough in a few hours to make up for several days or even weeks of small losses.

If you're winning at a casino where you fear specific trickery and you must leave the table for a few moments, make sure you have a friend who stays behind, never leaving the dice out of his sight. Also, observe new shooters who may appear at your table. Observe how they pick up the dice to toss them and whether they're lucky or unlucky. Always make sure that no shooter rearranges or slides the dice when tossing them. If you're at an honest casino no such actions will be allowed by the management.

Something else which plays a great role when shooting Craps is geometry. If you're not lucky at the spot where you're standing, you should move and shoot the dice from the opposite side of the table, if there is available space. Also, a quick shuffle of all the dice may change your luck. When you're not lucky and you are shooting, strength used in your tosses should vary. But when your luck is holding, don't change anything you're doing.

My favorite and quickest way to win at Craps was mentioned in the beginning of this book. If a player follows my instructions, and doubles up on his bets, his winnings are assured, provided that his stake is sufficient and he doesn't increase his wagers to extremes. Any reasonably astute player can win by doubling up on Don't Pass and Don't Come bets if he follows all the instructions. Most of my winnings were at unpatronized tables, however, where I was the only customer, and the only player tossing the dice. (The only time I suggest doubling up on the size of your wagers when losing is when betting on the Don't Come.)

I can conjure a vision of a majority of players following the suggestions I've made. And they always observe the most iron law of all: money management is the key to winning. This law cannot be invoked often enough.

Chapter 12

The Comp

Through the years I have stayed and gambled at almost every major hotel in Las Vegas. I have played other casinos in Reno, Lake Tahoe, and Atlantic City. Some of these places are the biggest and the most widely known resorts in the U.S. At these hotels my action was appreciated and the accommodations were always on a grand scale.

From the moment I walked in, my room, food, and beverage was comped by shift bosses, casino marketing executives, even vice presidents. (At some hotels I've been comped directly by the owner.) Most of the time a single room was satisfactory, but there were times when elegant master suites with spacious accommodations were offered. The gourmet cuisine was excellent and memorable. Most shows I have seen once, some twice, as the entertainers are among the best available in the country. All this was for free, each time I gambled at the top casinos. My only obligation was to sign the tab and pay the tips. My gambling was usually around the clock—more hours than any casino could expect. My female escorts were welcome to attend any performance in town, but they may never forgive me for refusing to join them at the show rooms. The desert sun and the swimming pools rarely attracted me. In nearly three decades, I did actually swim a total of less than a dozen times. If certain of my girl friends had not insisted that I join them at the pool, I probably would have never taken time off from the tables. Most certainly, the action attracted me more than any of the many lavish social evenings, which most people who visit such resorts rush to enjoy. My companions complained that we were not living normal lives.

"What good is a master suite if you only use it once a day...and that's to shower, shave, or change clothes?" a female friend once asked. "A meal or two per day...and you rush back to the tables for several hours of crazy action!"

To her way of thinking, she was on target. On my list, however, she was classified among the top of complaining female companions. I was aware that I was expected to spend hours with her at the restaurants, the shows, by the pool, and in our room. But my playing periods, at high stakes, is what brought the comp and provided the luxury surrounding her. In addition, my money management—which most commonly requires several hours to effectively pay off—required constant attention.

This part was always difficult to explain to most ladies. According to their understanding of casino comping, I was expected to bet for a limited period and spend the rest of the time entertaining them.

The comp is also another gamble. When a casino comps a particular player and his guest, the expense which accumulates in a few days usually runs in the thousands. During those few days the casino is banking mostly on the double-six or the double-Aces—whichever of those combinations it happens to bar—to make up for the comp expenses, pay for the overhead, and, of course, eventually profit from the freebies. When a player is fully comped he's banking on his money management and a few good luck sequences to survive the minus odds and perhaps win a few thousand while living royally. Thus, a casino operation presents a luxurious environment at no charge, for a few hours of play daily—usually four—at a standard or comfortable rate of wagering. If a person is planning to gamble seriously, the full comp should be considered a plus to his gambling stake. The only time the comp can become harmful to a gambler is when he's losing. In explanation, when a bettor is losing he should be free of the obligation rule, which is to play enough to cover the comp. My advice is, sure, take advantage of the comp. If you're losing stop gambling for a while. Almost every time I disregarded this rule I lost large sums. Since many times I gambled on a grand-scale, it is no secret that a single bet I wagered and lost could have easily paid for all my expenses to Europe for a month or longer.

One thing is certain: not a single casino forces a player to bet. However, if you prove to the hotel staff that you are a "strong" bettor and then ask to be comped, the offers you receive from casinos can become difficult to resist, particularly for high rollers; the accommodations are elegant.

At $100 per bet or higher, for a minimum playing period of approximately four hours daily, the costs of room, food and beverage, shows, and limo rides to other casinos have been made available at most resorts for many years. In certain smaller casino operations, for action of $25 per hand and up the hotel room has been picked up if the bettor played for a period of about four hours each day. The casino room-comp lessens obligations for the conservative bettor. This type of player may always ask a pit boss for food tickets to the coffee shop, buffet, or other dining. In most cases, a comped food ticket is offered. If the hotel where the bettor is staying is not very busy, during slow weeknights he may also ask to be comped at a show. Unless he asks, he can never be sure of the answer. Some hotels offer what they call a casino rate, which means that as long as the hotel guest is active in the casino, he or she is entitled to a room rate much lower than the standard cost.

For the $500 and up bettor, casinos will pick up round trip air flights for two. With a phone call, a limo may be arranged to pick you up at the airport. After you arrive at the hotel, all RF&B expenses will be complimentary.

Through the years I have been invited to various luxurious resorts as an MVP or VIP guest. The invitations offered such diverse vacations as an all expenses paid, RF&B, entertainment, boxing matches, golf tournaments, even swordfishing in San Juan, Puerto Rico. Many of those resorts offer excellent facilities and a relaxing gambling environment. To arrange for comped trips, all a guest needs to do is call a specific casino resort's 1-800 number. Casino marketing representatives will be more than happy to assist. The comp arrangement becomes much simpler after your playing average has entered the casino's computer system.

To simplify matters, during the last few years plastic membership cards are given to players who wish to have pit bosses keep track of their wagers, thus determining comp privileges. It's all a matter of qualification. If you play big, you'll leave the hotel with only tipping expenses. If you don't gamble, don't ask for very much—and be prepared to pay for all needs. Casino marketing will usually handle all comp transactions. Also, in the casino, any pit boss or shift boss can call and arrange for similar transactions to accommodate the player's RF&B comp privileges.

Many smaller casinos offer complimentary RF&B for their guests. In fact, several downtown Las Vegas places offer free drinks, food, and cigarettes for minimum play. Small action has earned bettors free meals when playing for relatively short periods at the tables. Some pit bosses may sign tickets for bettors who wish to walk to the bar for a few drinks to relax after the play. Small or large, complimentary services have been offered consistently for many years. But if a player doesn't request any of those comps offered, how else will his requests be fulfilled?

As long as you show up at the tables, "ask and most likely you shall receive" is the house rule at most casinos. In 1994 Las Vegas spent around $500 million on comps alone. (This figure was mentioned by CBS newsman Dan Rather on the program "48 Hours.") Before betting it's a good idea to hand your rating card to any pit boss so he can computerize your action. If you are not known in a particular casino, introduce yourself to a pit boss or even a shift boss. In most cases, you'll discover that they are friendly and extremely courteous. They obviously enjoy meeting new customers and will be more than happy to offer advice and information.

Epilogue

As I've noted in the preceding pages, I have gambled in a variety of casinos over the past three decades and participated frequently in private high stakes dice and most other gambling.

After considering the expenses of being a professional gambler—travel, tipping, even unrepaid loans I've made to other players (to say nothing of losing streaks)—my win total remains spectacular, even in my own eyes.

Large and small United States casinos are generally honest, especially the deluxe ones, which are the resorts originally coined as "carpet joints" by Ben ("Bugsy") Siegel, who might be called the father of modern Las Vegas. And remember that all the states where gambling is legal also have strict monitoring by gaming control boards. The house lives on the percentage, with slot machines being the foremost contributor to overhead.

To sum up: I love to gamble. And I'd like to quote another Greek gambler's memorable remark when interviewed: "The next best thing to playing and winning is playing and losing." That was said by Nick the Greek (Nicholas Dandolos). I might never quibble with that statement.

I am not advocating gambling, particularly for the high stakes for which I've played. But I trust (and hope) that the suggestions and instructions you've read might put you on a more even keel with the casino—and will contribute to making you a very knowledgeable gambler for the future.

I want you to win!

Gambling Books Ordering Information

Ask for any of the books listed below at your bookstore. Or to order direct from the publisher, call 1-800-447-BOOK (MasterCard or Visa), or send a check or money order for the books purchased (plus $4.00 shipping and handling for the first book ordered and $1.00 for each additional book) to Carol Publishing Group, 120 Enterprise Avenue, Dept. 51728, Secaucus, NJ 07094.

Beating the Wheel: The System That's Won More Than $6 Million, From Las Vegas to Monte Carlo by Russell T. Barnhart
$12.95 paper   0-8184-0553-8   (CAN $17.95)

Beat the House: Sixteen Ways to Win at Blackjack, Craps, Roulette, Baccarat and Other Table Games by Frederick Lembeck
$12.95 paper   0-8065-1607-0   (CAN $17.95)

Blackjack Your Way to Riches by Richard Albert Canfield
$12.95 paper   0-8184-0498-1   (CAN $17.95)

The Body Language of Poker: Mike Caro's Book of Tells by Mike Caro
$18.95 paper   0-89746-100-2   (CAN $26.95)

Caro on Gambling by Mike Caro
$6.95 paper   0-89746-029-4   (CAN $0.05)

The Cheapskate's Guide to Las Vegas: Hotels, Gambling, Food, Entertainment, and Much More by Connie Emerson
$9.95 paper   0-8065-1530-9   (CAN $13.95)

Darwin Ortiz on Casino Gambling: The Complete Guide to Playing and Winning by Darwin Ortiz
$12.95 paper   0-8184-0525-2   (CAN $17.95)

For Winners Only: The Only Casino Gambling Guide You'll Ever Need by Peter J. Andrews
$18.95 paper   0-8065-1728-X   (CAN $26.95)

Gambling Scams: How They Work, How to Detect Them, How to Protect Yourself by Darwin Ortiz
$11.95 paper   0-8184-0529-5   (CAN $15.95)

Gambling Times Guide to Blackjack by Stanley Roberts
$12.95 paper   0-89746-015-4   (CAN $17.95)

Gambling Times Guide to Craps by N.B. Winkless
$9.95 paper   0-89746-013-8   (CAN $13.95)

How to be Treated Like a High Roller by Robert Renneisen
$7.95 paper   0-8184-0556-2   (CAN $10.95)

How To Win at Casino Gaming Tournaments by Haven Earle Haley
$8.95 paper   0-89746-016-2   (CAN $11.95)

John Patrick's Advanced Craps
$18.95 paper   0-8184-0577-5   (CAN $26.95)

John Patrick's Blackjack
$12.95 paper   0-8184-0555-4   (CAN $17.95)

John Patrick's Craps
$14.95 paper   0-8184-0554-6   (CAN $20.95)

John Patrick's Slots
$12.95 paper   0-8184-0574-0   (CAN $17.95)

Million Dollar Blackjack by Ken Uston
$16.95 paper   0-89746-068-5   (CAN $23.95)

New Poker Games by Mike Caro
$5.95 paper   0-89746-040-5   (CAN $7.95)

Playing Blackjack as a Business by Lawrence Revere
$15.95 paper   0-8184-0064-1   (CAN $21.95)

Progression Blackjack: Exposing the Cardcounting Myth by Donald Dahl
$9.95 paper   0-8065-1396-9   (CAN $13.95)

Psyching Out Vegas: Winning Through Psychology in the Casinos of the World by Marvin Karlins, Ph.D.
$15.00 cloth   0-914314-03-3   (CAN $19.95)

Win at Video Poker: The Guide to Beating the Poker Machines by Roger Fleming
$9.95 paper   0-8065-1605-4   (CAN $13.95)

Winning at Slot Machines by Jim Regan
$5.95 paper   0-8065-0973-2   (CAN $7.95)

Winning Blackjack in Atlantic City and Around the World by Thomas Gaffney
$7.95 paper   0-8065-1178-8   (CAN $10.95)

Winning Blackjack Without Counting Cards by David S. Popik
$7.95 paper   0-8065-0963-5   (CAN $10.95)

(Prices subject to change; books subject to availability)